World Mythology: A Very Short Introduction

VERY SHORT INTRODUCTIONS are for anyone wanting a stimulating and accessible way into a new subject. They are written by experts, and have been translated into more than 45 different languages.

The series began in 1995, and now covers a wide variety of topics in every discipline. The VSI library currently contains over 700 volumes—a Very Short Introduction to everything from Psychology and Philosophy of Science to American History and Relativity—and continues to grow in every subject area.

Very Short Introductions available now:

ABOLITIONISM Richard S. Newman
THE ABRAHAMIC RELIGIONS
    Charles L. Cohen
ACCOUNTING Christopher Nobes
ADOLESCENCE Peter K. Smith
THEODOR W. ADORNO
    Andrew Bowie
ADVERTISING Winston Fletcher
AERIAL WARFARE Frank Ledwidge
AESTHETICS Bence Nanay
AFRICAN AMERICAN RELIGION
    Eddie S. Glaude Jr.
AFRICAN HISTORY John Parker
    and Richard Rathbone
AFRICAN POLITICS Ian Taylor
AFRICAN RELIGIONS Jacob K. Olupona
AGEING Nancy A. Pachana
AGNOSTICISM Robin Le Poidevin
AGRICULTURE Paul Brassley and
    Richard Soffe
ALEXANDER THE GREAT
    Hugh Bowden
ALGEBRA Peter M. Higgins
AMERICAN BUSINESS HISTORY
    Walter A. Friedman
AMERICAN CULTURAL HISTORY
    Eric Avila
AMERICAN FOREIGN RELATIONS
    Andrew Preston
AMERICAN HISTORY Paul S. Boyer
AMERICAN IMMIGRATION
    David A. Gerber
AMERICAN INTELLECTUAL
    HISTORY
    Jennifer Ratner-Rosenhagen

THE AMERICAN JUDICIAL SYSTEM
    Charles L. Zelden
AMERICAN LEGAL HISTORY
    G. Edward White
AMERICAN MILITARY HISTORY
    Joseph T. Glatthaar
AMERICAN NAVAL HISTORY
    Craig L. Symonds
AMERICAN POETRY David Caplan
AMERICAN POLITICAL HISTORY
    Donald Critchlow
AMERICAN POLITICAL PARTIES
    AND ELECTIONS L. Sandy Maisel
AMERICAN POLITICS
    Richard M. Valelly
THE AMERICAN PRESIDENCY
    Charles O. Jones
THE AMERICAN REVOLUTION
    Robert J. Allison
AMERICAN SLAVERY
    Heather Andrea Williams
THE AMERICAN SOUTH
    Charles Reagan Wilson
THE AMERICAN WEST Stephen Aron
AMERICAN WOMEN'S HISTORY
    Susan Ware
AMPHIBIANS T. S. Kemp
ANAESTHESIA Aidan O'Donnell
ANALYTIC PHILOSOPHY
    Michael Beaney
ANARCHISM Alex Prichard
ANCIENT ASSYRIA Karen Radner
ANCIENT EGYPT Ian Shaw
ANCIENT EGYPTIAN ART AND
    ARCHITECTURE Christina Riggs

Available soon:

For more information visit our website

www.oup.com/vsi/

David A. Leeming

WORLD MYTHOLOGY

A Very Short Introduction

OXFORD
UNIVERSITY PRESS

OXFORD
UNIVERSITY PRESS

Oxford University Press is a department of the University of Oxford.
It furthers the University's objective of excellence in research, scholarship,
and education by publishing worldwide. Oxford is a registered trade mark of
Oxford University Press in the UK and certain other countries.

Published in the United States of America by Oxford University Press
198 Madison Avenue, New York, NY 10016, United States of America.

Library of Congress Cataloging-in-Publication Data

Names: Leeming, David Adams, 1937- author.
Title: World mythology : a very short introduction / David Leeming.
Description: [New York] : Oxford University Press, [2022] |
Includes bibliographical references and index.
Identifiers: LCCN 2022018858 (print) | LCCN 2022018859 (ebook) |
ISBN 9780197548264 (paperback) | ISBN 9780197548288 (epub)
Subjects: LCSH: Mythology.
Classification: LCC BL312 .L443 2022 (print) | LCC BL312 (ebook) |
DDC 201/.3--dc23/eng/20220611
LC record available at https://lccn.loc.gov/2022018858
LC ebook record available at https://lccn.loc.gov/2022018859

1 3 5 7 9 8 6 4 2

Printed in the UK by Ashford Colour Press Ltd, Gosport, Hampshire,
on acid-free paper

For Margaret, Juliet, and Paul

Contents

List of illustrations

Definitions

In common parlance, a *myth* is a false but widespread belief. The superstition that walking under a ladder will result in catastrophic events is an example. Myth is also used in connection with sociopolitical movements or systems of thought. In the nineteenth century the myth of Manifest Destiny served to justify American expansion at the expense of Native Americans. Other such myths are that of the master race central to Nazi ideology and the dictatorship of the proletariat of Marxist communism. Myths such as the Oedipus and Elektra complexes are basic to Freudian psychology. Myth used in these ways refers to concepts and theories. Myth as used in this Very Short Introduction to world mythology refers to narratives involving extraordinary or supernatural events and characters widely accepted as truth in one sense or another by certain groups of people in the past or even in the present time. Most people would agree that stories of the Greek Olympians or Norse gods and heroes are, in this sense, myths. It can be argued that such myths contain or point to metaphorical truths, much as we might find some truth in the extraordinary events of our dreams.

In a more academic sense, *mythology* is the study of myths or of approaches to a more general concept we call myth. Mythology also refers to the collected myths of particular cultures—thus, Greek mythology, Egyptian mythology, Norse mythology, biblical mythology, or Hindu mythology, for instance. Studying these mythologies inevitably reveals something of the inner identity of the given cultures. A comparative consideration of the themes and priorities inherent in world mythology, the collection of cultural mythologies, leads to the exposure of mythological constructs that transcend cultures—constructs such as the deity myth, the creation myth, or the hero myth and the frequently present constructs such as the flood myth or the trickster myth. These constructs are, in effect, universal aspects of the dreams of a species realized in cultural clothes.

More often than not, myths tend to be what we would call religious narratives. Deity myths are religious by definition. Creation and flood myths always involve deities in relation to the world. Trickster and hero myths, although not necessarily overtly religious, serve as metaphors for the existence of both evil and the human psyche's drive to achieve a higher state of being.

Some of the figures and stories treated here will be familiar to most readers. Others will be unfamiliar. Some narratives come primarily from legends and folk tales but nevertheless contain strong mythic elements such as the miraculous conception, the sacred quest, or the descent to an underworld. The purpose for the inclusion of unfamiliar mythologies and mythologized folk material is to reveal both the cultural variety and the universality of the narratives and characters of which *world* mythology is composed.

Chapter 1
Deity

Paleolithic rock and cave art and burial sites indicate that since early in prehistory human beings have entertained the concept of a higher power that either creates life or orders it in some way. Since at least the Neolithic, artists and mythmakers have conceived of that power as deities, beings with human or animal characteristics, beings that usually are immortal and sometimes omnipresent and omniscient, or even omnipotent. There are sky gods who exist somehow outside our earthly experience, and there are earth deities who reside in our world. There are creator deities and earth/mother goddesses. There are storm gods and warrior gods; angry, vengeful gods and benevolent loving gods; gods who exist as innumerable spirits all around us. There are high gods who exist with other gods but stand out above the others and sometimes contain these others as aspects of themselves. And there are gods who exist alone above creation. Much of human history reflects the struggles between gods of these various types, represented by their followers, for dominance of cultures, nations, and even the world.

Until the rise of monotheism, deities were generally members of pantheistic families we call pantheons, such as those in ancient Mesopotamia, Egypt, and Greece, or they were less formal collections of spirits such as the Hopi *kachina*, the Japanese *kami*, or the Yoruba *orisha*.

Mesopotamia (Sumer): the Anunuki

Ancient Sumer, in what is now southern Iraq, is generally thought to be the first of the great civilizations to emerge from the Neolithic revolution. With the accelerated development of agriculture and animal husbandry came the parallel development in Sumer, beginning in about 4000 BCE, of large permanent settlements or cities and eventually writing, which is to say, history. And with these aspects of civilization came a priestly caste and the establishment of an organized mythology. That mythology, with its pantheon of gods, provided a metaphysical expression of the society's primary concerns, fertility, and governmental order. Much as Roman mythological figures were related to Greek ones, the Sumerian deities took related forms and new names in the mythologies of the Semitic peoples—the Akkadians, Babylonians, and Assyrians—who over the centuries replaced the Sumerians in Mesopotamia.

The father god of the Sumerians was An (Semitic Anu). His family of gods was known as the Anunuki. An, with his roaring thunder, was an embodiment of the sky. His wife Ki was Earth, whom he fertilized with his semen-rain. Both An and Ki were children of the mother goddess Nammu. An was associated primarily with the Sumerian city of Uruk.

More important than the somewhat distant An was his son, the storm god Enlil (Elil). Enlil controlled the *me*, the elements of Sumerian divine order. It was he who gave divine authority to Sumerian kings. Enlil's city was Nippur. His sometimes wife was the great mother goddess Ninhursaga, who embodied earthly fertility, childbirth, and the seasons and whose sacred sign included the uterus of a cow, associating her with the even more ancient figure of the Neolithic cow goddess. Among Enlil's many offspring was the moon god Nanna (Sin), who presided over the city of Ur.

A son of An and the riverbed goddess Nammu ("Lady Vulva") was Enki (Ea), whose city was Eridu and whose name revealed him as lord (*en*) of earth (*ki*). He lived in the underground sweet waters of the southern marshlands. A wise god with trickster characteristics, Enki had an insatiable sexual appetite, which made him an apt embodiment of fertility. Myths about Enki support his role as the guardian of the important irrigation principles of Sumer. One myth tells how, even though he was married to another, Enki directed his semen into the womb of the earth mother Ninhursaga. When the goddess gave birth to the beautiful goddess Nimmu, Enki directed his semen to her womb, and she gave birth to still another goddess, Ninkurra ("mistress of the land"). Enki then impregnated Ninkurra, resulting in the birth of Uttu ("vegetation"). Enki hoped to pour his semen into Uttu's womb, but Ninhursaga advised the girl to resist the god until he promised to bring her fruits and vegetables from the dry lands. This Enki did. After Enki entered Uttu, Ninhursaga wiped excess semen from the girl's body and used it to make new plants.

A dominant figure in Sumerian mythology was the goddess Inanna, who later was known as Ishtar in the Mesopotamian Semitic cultures. She was the daughter of either the father god An, the high god Enlil, or Enki. The myth of her marriage with the shepherd king Dumuzi (Tammuz) gave metaphysical justification for kingship and for a sacred marriage tradition in which kings and representatives of the goddess were ritually married in the city of Uruk, Inanna's cult center.

A more important aspect of the Inanna–Dumuzi myth is Inanna's representation of the land itself and its fertility. In the myth, Utu the sun god, whose role was to supervise growth on earth, tells his newly adolescent twin sister, Inanna, that she is now ripe for marriage and love. The farmer Enkimdu and the shepherd Dumuzi both court the goddess. After she chooses the shepherd, her mother, the reed goddess Ningal, tells Inanna to "open your house" to Dumuzi. When Inanna does open the door to Dumuzi, the bride and groom are overcome by passion. Inanna calls out:

> My vulva, the horn,
> The Boat of Heaven,
> Is full of eagerness like the young moon.
> My untilled land lies fallow.

And Dumuzi answers:

> I, Dumuzi, the king, will plow your vulva.

A curious Inanna myth is that of her descent to the underworld ruled over by her sister Ereshkigal. If Inanna is a goddess of love and fertility, Ereshkigal is her opposite, a goddess of infertility and death. Inanna determines that to fully understand life, the overall process of fertility, she must examine the darkness of the underworld. Before leaving on her journey, Inanna instructs her faithful companion Ninshubur to prepare a mourning ceremony for her and, should she fail to return, to approach Enlil, the moon god Nanna, or Enki for help. Like the plants of her fields that die in winter, Inanna abandons the trappings of her glory as she approaches the underworld. At the gates of her sister's realm, she demands admittance, claiming that she has come for the funeral of Gugalanna, the Bull of Heaven. The Bull of Heaven is a figure traditionally associated with the great goddess of the earlier Neolithic period. In Sumer he was a symbol of the kings of Uruk and an astrological figure (Taurus) who disappeared in winter and returned in the spring. Inanna's descent for his funeral represents her association with the life, death, and resurrection in the agricultural process that she embodies. Ereshkigal demands that if Inanna is to enter her underground kingdom of death and infertility, she must abandon all of her remaining queenly ornaments and appear naked before her. Inanna challenges Ereshkigal, and her powerlessness in the underworld is clear when her sister hangs her up to die and dry like a piece of meat.

Back in Uruk, after three days and nights since the queen's departure, Ninshubur, following her mistress's instructions, approaches Inanna's relatives for help. Only Enki, the wise god, who understands Inanna's importance to Sumerian life and fertility, agrees to help. Because his home is the underground waters, he is closer than the others to the underworld and determines what must be done to liberate the goddess. Enki creates two beings, the Plant of Life and the Water of Life, from mud under his fingernails and sends them to the underworld, where he tells them they are to give comfort to Ereshkigal, who constantly suffers the pains of negative, unproductive childbirth. In return, the two beings are to request from Ereshkigal the body of Inanna. This they do, and after receiving the body, they are able to revive it. The gods of the underworld, however, demand a substitute for the revived goddess. When Inanna returns home, having regained her clothing, her jewelry, and all the symbols of her power, she finds her husband Dumuzi apparently enjoying his kingship without his wife. He is horrified when Inanna announces that he is to be her substitute in the underworld. Only when Dumuzi's sister offers to spend six months of each year there for him is he allowed the other six months reigning in Uruk with the great goddess, performing his sacred kingship role as fertilizer of the land.

Egypt: The Ogdoad and the Ennead

The mythology of ancient Egypt resembles that of Sumer in that it places a great deal of emphasis on a sacred kingship related to elements of its pantheons. It also shares with Sumer an understandable concern with fertility. In Egypt this concern is based in part in the death and resurrection process made real in the annual flooding of the Nile. Egyptian mythology's most notable characteristic is its concern with death and the afterlife, especially in connection with the god king Osiris, his sister-wife, Isis, and their son, Horus. As symbolic vehicles for metaphysical thought about the nature of existence, these and other Egyptian deities formed pantheons that varied somewhat according to different cult centers. But, in general, the centers were in agreement as to the nature and the functions of their deities.

Archeological evidence points to a mother goddess cult featuring the goddesses Hathor, Neith, Maat, and Isis, among others. This would be in keeping with the Neolithic goddess cults that existed in such early sites as Çatal Hüyük and Hacilar and elsewhere. It is not until the Early Dynastic period, beginning in about 3100 BCE, when Upper and Lower Egypt were united at Memphis, under King Narmer (also known as Aha or Menes), forming the first great historical nation-state, that the more formal pantheons of Egyptian mythology began to come into being. This was shortly after the early development of hieroglyphic writing. By that time, the Egyptian concept of kingship was already based on the direct connection between the king and a god, usually either Horus, the falcon-headed sun god, or his enemy, Set (Seth).

During the Old Kingdom (ca. 2700–2190 BCE), pantheons took full theological form at the various cult centers, such as those at Memphis, Heliopolis, and Khemenu (Hermopolis), near what is now Cairo. The creator god Ptah stood at the head of the Memphis pantheon. His wife was the lioness goddess Sekhmet. In the Hermopolic pantheon, Ptah became Amun. This pantheon was known as the Ogdoad ("the Eight"), composed of four couples representing the primordial forces of nature. Amun and Amaunet were the invisible power, Huh and Hauhet were infinity, Kuk and Kauhet were darkness, and Nun and Naunet were the primal waters.

In Heliopolis, generally the dominant center, Atum ("the whole One") was the creator god combining male and female. Later he would be assimilated into the sun god Re or Atum-Re, or Amun-Re. Atum was the founder of the Ennead ("the Nine"). He produced Shu and Tefnut (Air and Moisture), who in turn produced Geb and Nut (Earth and Sky), who were the parents of Osiris and his wife, Isis, and Set and his wife, Nephthys.

The Middle Kingdom (2050–1756 BCE) was ruled primarily from the Upper (Southern) Egyptian city of Thebes (Waset, modern Luxor and Karnak). Amun-Re, the ram-headed sun god, an assimilation of earlier king gods, became the dominant deity. Still later, in the Amarna period (1353–1327 BCE), the pharaoh Amenhotep IV, married to Nefertiti, disassociated himself from Amun-Re and the other gods and changed his name to Akhenaton in honor of Aten, whom he established as a de facto monotheistic or at least monist or monolatristic sun god, represented as a sun disk. At Akhenaton's death, Amun-Re and the other gods were restored to their former positions of religious dominance under Akhenaton's son, Tutankhamun ("King Tut").

Deities who maintained importance essentially throughout the history of ancient Egypt were Osiris and his wife, Isis. It is their story that most clearly reflects the centrality of Egyptian deities in the concepts of fertility, the sacred kingship, and the meaningful afterlife.

Osiris and Isis were children of Geb and Nut in the Heliopolis Ennead. Although Osiris was probably worshipped as a god-king in the predynastic period, his cult became prominent later, during the Fifth Dynasty (2494–2345 BCE), and remained central to funerary and kingship succession rituals and theology until well into the Roman period. He is usually depicted as a mummy wearing a crown and carrying a crook as King of the Dead. In death, pharaohs became Osiris; in life they were an embodiment of Osiris and Isis's son, Horus. Isis also remained a popular deity until the end of Egyptian civilization. She, too, was clearly associated with fertility, the afterlife, and the sacred kingship. As the goddess of the throne and mother of Horus, she was the theological mother of each pharaoh.

1. An Egyptian terra cotta figure of the great Middle Eastern goddess Isis–Aphrodite (second century CE) stands proudly in celebration of her power and fertility.

The complex myth of Osiris and Isis can be pieced together from elements of the ancient Pyramid and Coffin texts (2400–2040 BCE), written on pyramid walls and coffins, and various later writings of the Greco-Roman period, especially those of Plutarch (first century CE). The texts agree generally that Osiris was a god-king of Egypt who was killed by his brother, Set and revived by his wife, Isis sufficiently to make the conception of Horus possible. In some accounts, Osiris was dismembered by Set and thrown into the Nile. With the help of Anubis, the jackal-headed god of mummification, and the Ibis-headed Thoth, god of wisdom and magic and the inventor of writing, the parts of the dismembered god were retrieved from the river. Through spells initiated by Isis and her sister (Set's wife) Nephthys, spells such as those found in the *Book of the Coming Forth by Day* (Book of the dead, 1550 BCE), Osiris was at least partially revived and was able to impregnate Isis before leaving for the underworld.

Osiris's kingship in the underworld is related to the resurrection of life in the crops that resulted from the death of life and its return in the annual flooding and subsequent retreat of the Nile. In this connection, models of the god's body parts, perhaps especially his genitals, were ritually planted along the Nile to ensure the annual flood-based fertility so important to a desert-bound country. The Nile itself was thought to be related to the bodily fluids of the dead Osiris.

In the New Kingdom (1550–712 BCE) books relating to the underworld, the sun god Re went to the place where Osiris was buried and entered the dead god's soul, allowing him to live again as the judge of all those who die and seek a place in his underworld. By the New Kingdom, Osiris, Isis, and Horus were a divine family with Isis achieving dominance as a "Mother of God" figure, foreshadowing the role of Mary in the Christian Holy Family.

Greece and Rome: the Olympians and their ancestors

The gods and goddesses of ancient Greece, as revealed by Homer, Hesiod, and others, are much more related to human life than the gods of Sumer and Egypt. The Greek pantheon performs what is, in effect, a large-scale soap opera reflecting the worst in human behavior. Known as the Olympians, because they lived on Mount Olympus, the family headed by Zeus resembles dysfunctional families in the human world—especially privileged ones—and reflects a humanistic culture's skeptical, ironic, and fatalistic attitude toward deities and life in general. The stories of these gods expose them as arbitrary, cruel, and self-serving, not only among themselves but also in their many relationships with humans. At best their activities are merely comic.

That the Olympians were the way they were is not surprising given what the Greek myths tell of their immediate ancestors. Hesiod tells how the great goddess Gaia (Earth) was abused by her husband, Ouranos (Sky) to such an extent that, in desperation, she plotted with her son Kronos (Time) to strike out against the abuser. In what in the early twenty-first century might be called a supremely Freudian act, Kronos castrated his father with a sickle provided by his mother and took control of the universe as leader of the Titans. But Kronos inherited his father's abusive nature and swallowed each of the children he fathered with his sister-wife Rhea. With Rhea's help, her son Zeus avoided being swallowed and eventually was able to free his siblings and defeat his father for the kingship of heaven. Zeus and his brothers and sisters were the older generation of Olympians: Hestia, Demeter, Poseidon, Hera, and Hades (although Hades lived "under the earth").

As head of the Olympian family, Zeus was a leader with limitless power, symbolized by his thunderbolt. And he was the ultraphilanderer. He had sexual relations with mortals and immortals, both male and female. Sometimes he used disguise—

for instance, a bull or swan—to accomplish his predatory goals without his wife's knowledge. As an eagle, he abducted the human boy Ganymede and carried him off to Olympus. As a swan, he raped Leda. Zeus had several children. The Olympian goddess Athena was conceived in the Titaness Metis but was born from Zeus's head as the goddess of wisdom. The god Dionysos (only rarely included in the list of Olympians) was fathered by Zeus in the mortal Semele but preserved at her death in his thigh for eventual birth. Dionysos was an outsider, the central figure in an ancient mystery cult that involved frenetic dancing, sexuality, wine, and the celebration of the earthly—as opposed to heavenly— cycles of death and rebirth. Aspects of the cult are revealed in Euripides's play, *The Bacchae*.

Other children of Zeus were Apollo and Artemis by another Titaness, Leto. By the nymph Maia, he fathered Hermes. Zeus did have children by his wife, Hera. These were the warrior god Ares and the blacksmith Hephaistos (although one story has it that Hera conceived Hephaistos parthenogenetically—that is, without Zeus's help). Zeus also was said by some to be the father of the goddess Aphrodite, though others said she was conceived in the sea by the "foam" flowing from the severed genitals of Ouranos.

The rest of the Olympian family, except for Hestia, who sat quietly by the Olympian hearth, followed in the pattern of privileged dysfunction. Zeus's brother, the sea god Poseidon, forced himself on his sister, the agricultural goddess Demeter. The underworld god Hades abducted his niece, Demeter's daughter, Persephone. Demeter searched for her daughter and eventually secured a promise that she would be returned to earth for part of each year. These events provided the basis for an agricultural mystery cult known as the Eleusinian Mysteries.

As for the rest of the family, Zeus's son Ares had an affair with his sister or stepsister Aphrodite, the family vamp. The couple were caught by Aphrodite's husband, the hunchback Hephaistos,

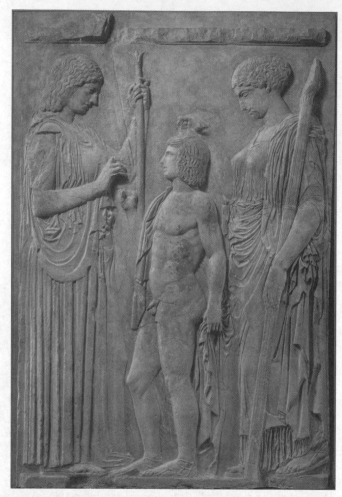

2. A fragment of a marble relief dating from between 440 and 430 BCE comes from the sanctuary of Demeter in Eleusis. The goddess Demeter holds a scepter, and on the right, her daughter, Persephone holds a long torch. In the center is a demigod, Triptolemus, whom Demeter sends around Greece to teach people the art of agriculture.

forever after a symbol of cuckolds. Zeus's wife, Hera stood for wronged wives who understandably became suspicious and nagging. She usually applied her ire to the women Zeus had seduced, having little power over the patriarchal dominance her husband possessed. Zeus's son Hermes was generally mild-mannered, but he could take advantage of his privileged position, as, for instance, when he raped the fleet-footed maiden Apemosyne, using trickery to catch her. Hermes's sister Artemis was a confirmed virgin and a hunter. She took terrible vengeance on males who angered her, including the poor hunter Actaeon who inadvertently came upon her bathing and was punished by being turned into a stag whom his own dogs then tore to pieces.

Artemis's brother Apollo, god of arts and prophecy, and the goddess Athena were less dysfunctional than other members of their family. Apollo's love affairs, for instance, tended to be failures and thus to make him more sympathetic. He loved the Spartan boy Hyacinth, but as they were throwing discuses together, one of Apollo's discs killed the boy. Apollo also loved the nymph Daphne, but she managed to escape him, according to the Roman poet Ovid, by being turned into a tree. Athena was masculinized as a virgin warrior. She had a fondness for favorite human heroes such as Odysseus and Perseus.

If Athena represents a somewhat positive relationship between gods and humans, most of the Greek deities direct human life according to arbitrary, conflicting, and fickle impulses. Nowhere is this clearer than in Homer's *Iliad* and *Odyssey*, for instance, where divine actions manipulate, amplify, and accentuate a fatalistic and tragic helplessness at the basis of human existence.

It is commonplace to equate Roman mythology to that of Greece. The head Roman god is Jupiter, a cognate of the Greek Zeus. Juno is Hera, Mars is Ares, Vulcan is Hephaistos, Diana is Artemis, Mercury is Hermes, Minerva is Athena, Venus is Aphrodite, Vesta is Hestia, Pluto is Hades, Ceres is Demeter, Neptune is Poseidon, and Apollo is still Apollo.

In fact, Roman mythology attaches different meanings and levels of importance to its version of the Olympians. The Roman pantheon by the time of the Republic was an amalgam of Etruscan and Latin tribal as well as Greek ideas. Juno, who in Greece was the ever-jealous Hera, the nagging jealous wife of Zeus, became in Rome a version of the Mediterranean Great Mother goddess, who ruled with Jupiter and Minerva on Rome's Capitoline Hill. Ares, the war god in Greece, as Mars took on qualities of an agricultural god in Rome. Hestia became a version of the Indo-European fire deity supported by the Vestal Virgins. And the vampish and highly sexual Aphrodite became the much more sedate mother of the Rome-founding Trojan hero Aeneas. As the de facto patroness of Rome, she had something of the status that Athena had in Athens.

Norselands (Iceland): the Vanir and the Aesir

"Norse" mythology is the mythology of the Norsemen, who lived in Scandinavia and other parts of northern Europe in the early Middle Ages. As raiders and settlers of Britain, Ireland, Iceland, and other northern European areas, they are more popularly known as Vikings. Their Germanic language, Old Norse, is the source of present-day Scandinavian languages. The myths of the Norse people influenced those we associate with the Anglo-Saxons and Germans, myths such as those contained in the Anglo-Saxon epic of *Beowulf* and the German epic the *Niebelungenlied*. The primary source for Norse mythology, however, is Icelandic texts known as the *Younger Edda*, or *Prose Edda*, compiled by the Icelandic statesman and scholar Snorri Sturluson in about 1220 CE. Sturluson's work is based on much older stories from the oral tradition and from the *Elder Edda* or *Poetic Edda*, written down between the ninth and twelfth centuries CE.

The Norse deities belong to two pantheons. The older of the pantheons was that of the Vanir. These were fertility gods and goddesses associated with water and earth. The most famous of the Vanir were Freyr and Freya, offspring of Njord the sea god and the giant Skadi. Freya contains within herself the power of fecundity, the miracle of sexuality and birth. She is also a goddess of war. Not surprisingly, she has many sexual liaisons. Once she gave herself to four dwarves in return for her primary symbol of fertility, the necklace of the Brisings. Freyr, often depicted with a large phallus, is a god of earthly fertility and the sun. Freyr, Freya, and their father, Njord, form a fertility trinity.

The Vanir fought for many years with a younger pantheon, the Aesir. If the Vanir were deities of the earth, the Aesir were warrior deities of the sky, living in a Norse version of Mount Olympus called Asgard. The Aesir were led by the high god and "All Father" Odin (German Wotan) from his palace, Valhalla ("Hall of the Slain"). Odin entertained fallen heroes there. In some ways, he was a mysterious god associated with magic runes that contained ultimate meaning. He once hung on the world tree Yggdrasill for nine days in an act of self-sacrifice, trying to understand the runes. Like Jesus in the New Testament story, Odin was pierced there by a spear. On the tree, he died; he was "given to Odin, / myself given to myself." In this hanging—a death and rebirth—Odin acted out a ritual associated with his cult. Odin's consort was Frigg, goddess of love. Thor, the powerful god of the thunderbolt, rivaled Odin in power. Tyr was god of war. Heimdall guarded the bridge leading to Asgard. Balder was a much-loved god who died because of the treachery of the trickster god Loki.

Although the Vanir and Aesir fought a terrible war, they eventually reconciled and formed a single pantheon under the rule of Odin, until the "End of the Gods" and the world in the apocalypse known as Ragnarok.

Celtic (Ireland/Wales): the Tuatha De Danann and the family of Don

Celtic deities form pantheons of varying degrees of cohesion in the European mainland and especially in Ireland and Wales. The

Roman conquerors of Gaul tended to see the continental Celtic pantheon in connection with their own gods. In his *de Bello Gallico*, Julius Caesar assumed that the Gallic god of arts, crafts, and journeys was, in fact, a version of the Roman Mercury (Greek Hermes). A disease-curing god was really Apollo, a god of war was Mars (Ares), and the head god was Jupiter (Zeus).

In various texts complied by Irish monks beginning in the sixth century CE, an ancient Irish Celtic pantheon emerges. The *Lebor Gabala Erenn* (The book of taking of Ireland, or The book of invasions), for instance, tells of several groups who arrived in Ireland, beginning with the people of Noah's granddaughter, Cesair, and including the invasion of a family of gods, the Tuatha De Danann, the people of the mother goddess Danu. The Tuatha invasion preceded that of the Gaels, the Sons of Mil, the mythical ancestors of the present-day Irish. But even after that invasion, the Tuatha remained in Ireland as the *Sidhe*, fairy people of folklore, who are said to live in mounds under the Irish hills to this day.

In their days of great power, the Tuatha were a pantheon in the tradition of divine families such as those of Sumer and Greece. Although little is known of Danu, their mother goddess progenitor, the Tuatha represent a common Indo-European tripartite arrangement of sovereign/priest, warrior, and artisan. The god Lugh contains the tripartite arrangement within himself. He is a druidic priest, a great warrior, and a master artist. Mac ind (Og) or Aongus (Oenghus) is known as a god who is good at everything and is the son of the All Father Dagda, a supreme representative of both the priestly and the warrior class. His daughter is Brigid, a healer and a patroness of the arts and crafts. Later she would be assimilated by Christianity into Brigid of Kildare, whose sacred fire protected Vestal Virgins. Goibhniu was the smith god, and Donn, the Brown One, was a god of death. Ogma was a Hercules-like warrior, and Dian Cecht was a great healer who provided King Nuada's arm, severed in battle, with a silver arm. Nuada's wife was the warrior queen Macha.

The Tuatha established their high court at Tara. Nuada became king there and later ceded his power to Lugh, who used magical druidic powers to defeat enemies known as the Fomorians, led by the giant Balar, who killed both Nuada and Queen Macha before Lugh, like the biblical David, killed him with his slingshot.

To the extent that there is a Welsh pantheon related to the Irish Tuatha De Danann, it is found in a collection of tales known as the *Mabinogion* found in fourteenth-century manuscripts based on much earlier oral narratives. The Welsh pantheon is the Family of Don, Don being the earth goddess equivalent of the Irish Danu. The *Mabinogion* is divided into four "branches," the fourth of which is primarily concerned with the Family of Don. The dominant figure here is Lleu, who resembles the Irish Lugh. Other figures are two sons of Don, Gwydion and Gilfaethy, who are known for their magical powers. They overcome Lleu's mother's oath that her son will never marry into a race "now on earth" by creating Blodeuwedd from various flowers, and she becomes Lleu's wife. Blodeuwedd plots against her husband when she falls in love with another man and causes Lleu's death. Gwydion's magic, however, revives the god.

Celtic deities are unusual in that they tend to lack immortality or the power of Greek or Indian deities, for instance. They exist somewhere between the category of hero and god.

India: the faces of Brahman

The gods and goddesses of India have their source in the ancient Vedic texts, especially the *Rig-Veda*, composed in about 1500 BCE. The concept of deity as it has developed in India takes many forms depending on the various schools of classical Hinduism. Many Hindus are especially devoted to one of the gods of the Trimurti, which is made up of Shiva, Vishnu, and Brahma, although over time, Devi, the great goddess in her many iterations, has tended to become more important and Brahma less so.

In the original Trimurti, Brahma is the creator of the universe, Vishnu is its preserver, and Shiva is its destroyer leading to its recreation. Each of these gods has a spouse, who represents the god's *shakti* or energizing material power. Generally, Saraswati, goddess of learning and the arts, the founder of Sanskrit, the sacred language that articulates creation, is Brahma's wife. Siva's wife is Parvati, goddess of love and fertility. She is the mother of the popular elephant-headed god Ganesha. Often she is depicted in sexual embrace with Shiva, his sacred phallus (*lingam*) in her sacred vagina (*yoni*), representing the god in union with his shakti. Vishnu's wife and shakti is Sri Lakshmi, goddess of good fortune and prosperity. Each of these goddesses may be said to be aspects of Maha-Devi, the great goddess.

For worshippers of Shiva (Shaivites), Shiva is the primary god; he is Nataraja, Lord of the Dance, the ultimate yoga-ascetic, whose dance represents the breathing of the universe, the process of life, including its destruction, the death without which there can be no regeneration. As Shiva whirls, the living world is revealed in the flashes of light created by the dance movements. These flashes, in turn, are destroyed by the dance's violent turnings. Shiva has four arms. In his raised right hand is an hourglass/drum, symbolizing sound in the rhythm of the life dance. It is through sound that understanding is transmitted. In the raised left hand the dancer holds fire, the crucial element in the creative sacrificial destruction in the cosmic cycle of existence. The lower right hand presents the sign of peace. The lower left hand points to the left foot, which is raised, symbolizing devotion and release.

Devotion (*bhakti*), practiced by worshippers of Vishnu (Vaishnavites), stresses god's preservation of the universal order. Vishnu, too, has four arms. He carries a conch and his flaming discus weapon and the lotus. He rides on the eagle Garuda. He becomes incarnate as needed in the world by taking the form of various avatars, most famously Rama and Krishna.

Krishna's foster mother Yashoda saw the whole universe when she examined the inside of her son's mouth. And in the great religious text, the Bhagavad Gita, Krishna reveals himself as Vishnu, the personal embodiment of primal supreme power. Rama, the principal character of the great epic, the *Ramayana*, represents perfect adherence to the Hindu concept of *dharma* or social obligation. His wife, Sita, the avatar of Vishnu's wife Sri Lakshmi, embodies the perfect Hindu wife in the context of the same principle.

The goddess Devi in her many incarnations is the object of devotion for Shakvas (shakti). Two incarnations, Kali and Durga, are among the most popular. Both are sometimes wives of Shiva, but on their own they wield immense power. Durga, the "inaccessible," is the multiarmed warrior goddess. It is she who saves the gods and the universe itself by killing the buffalo demon Mahisa. Kali, the dark goddess of destruction, with her bloody fangs and human heads worn as a necklace, is a logical wife for Shiva as the destroyer. Kali sprang from the head of the angry Durga. Sometimes depicted dancing on the body of Shiva, she represents the central importance of sacrifice in the cyclical process of life. Whereas Shiva's destructive power is cosmic, Kali's is of this world. Her name is derived from the Sanskrit word *kala*, meaning "time."

The concept of divinity in Hinduism and its Vedic sources may certainly be said, like the deity concept in Sumer, Egypt, and Greece, to be polytheistic. There are literally thousands of Hindu gods. But it is also true that devotees of Shiva, and those of Vishnu and Devi, see their gods in a monist sense, as the Supreme Being, containing all other gods. The monistic tendency takes a still more radical step in the concept of Brahman (not to be confused with the old creator god Brahma) as understood by practitioners of various forms of Vedanta (literally the culmination or "end of the Vedas"). Essentially based on ideas contained in the Upanishads (800–200 BCE), Vedanta sees Brahman as the Absolute, present everywhere and nowhere, the undifferentiated reality underlying all apparent reality, including in the personal inner life as Atman, the Self, or Brahman within. Although seeing deity in all things might be called a pantheistic understanding, in Vedanta the concept of Brahman comes close to what many would call monotheism.

Israel/Palestine/Arabia: Yahweh/God/Allah

The tendency in world mythology to create a unified deity culminates in the monotheistic god of Judaism, Christianity, and Islam. The god of the ancient Hebrews or Israelites, too holy to name, was expressed in the form of the tetragrammaton, YHVH, usually vocalized as Yahweh. This god first appears as the Creator in the book of Genesis in the Hebrew Bible. At first Yahweh may well have been a god among many for the Hebrews, or at least a god of many names. Like the Canaanite gods Baal and El and other Middle Eastern gods, he was a storm or weather god (some say a volcano god) who controlled the fertility of what was a farming culture. He was particularly devoted to the Israelites, his "chosen people," and would mercilessly kill their enemies. When the Egyptian army followed the Hebrews out of Egypt with the intention of killing or recapturing them, Yahweh drowned the whole army in the Red Sea. The attraction of polytheism, however, was strong in the land of Canaan, the biblical "promised land" of the Hebrew/Israelites. It was not until the time of the exile in Babylon and the re-establishment of Israel in the sixth century BCE that monotheism, as opposed to polytheism or monolatry, was fully established in what became Judaism.

The Christian understanding of "God" in the New Testament addition to the Bible, while recognizing that God is one and the same as the Yahweh of the Hebrew scripture, takes on a different tone. The New Testament God is the loving and merciful "Our Father in Heaven," whose gift to the world is his "son," Jesus. For Christians, this god is the divine organizing force of the universe (Logos, the Word) experienced in three essential dimensions. He is the Creator, he is incarnate as Jesus, and he inhabits life as the Holy Spirit. The unique vision of deity here is the belief that God enters the world as Jesus and experiences human life in all its pain, including death, which he overcomes in resurrection.

As a dying god figure, Jesus has mythological relatives around the world. The dying god motif usually involves sacrifice and resurrection. Osiris in Egypt is a dying and resurrected god, as are Attis in Phrygia, the goddess Hainuwele in Ceram Indonesia, Baal in Canaan and Dionysos in the Orphic tradition in Greece, and Adonis in Greece and Phoenicia. In Norse mythology the much loved Balder is a dying god, and the supreme god Odin dies symbolically as he hangs on the world tree. Sir James Frazer and others have argued that the dying god motif is associated with the cycles of agriculture related to the seasons and fertility. Not surprisingly, then, the dying god is often associated with a female figure. Cybele is Attis's consort and mother in Phrygia, the goddess Anat helps to resurrect Baal in Canaan, and Isis does the same for Osiris in Egypt.

The Abrahamic god is nearly always referred to as a male. He is unlike other gods, however, in that he has no wife. Metaphorically, Yahweh is married to Israel and God is married to the church, but in Christianity the latent power of the goddess in a patriarchal religion is expressed in the figure of the Virgin Mary. Mary becomes a de facto goddess. Not only is she said to have conceived and given birth to Jesus while preserving her virgin state, but also the church in later doctrines proclaims the Immaculate Conception of Mary herself—that is, a sexless and sinless conception—and also establishes Mary's Assumption into heaven to sit with God as Regina Caeli, Queen of Heaven.

In Islam, the deity is Allah, a word that means simply "the god" (al-lah). Allah was the name of the dominant god among many in an ancient Arabic Meccan pantheon. This was the god who introduced himself to Abram (later Abraham), the father of all three "Abrahamic" monotheistic religions. Allah clarified his existence in the holy book, the Quran, dictated via the angel Jibril (Gabriel) to Allah's human "messenger" and primary prophet, Muhammed. The ultimate message of the holy book is, "There is no god greater than Allah." Allah as understood by Muslims is somewhat different than the Yahweh of the Jews or the God of Christians in that he is more a Brahman-like celestial power than a personal god who interacts directly with his people.

In all three Abrahamic visions of the supreme power, supernatural events—what many would call myths—play large roles. For example, Yahweh opens the Red Sea for the Hebrews to march through to freedom, Jesus performs miracles in his "father's" name and rises from the dead, and Muhammed flies on the winged mule al-Buraq from Mecca to Jerusalem and mounts the ladder to the seven heavens to experience the divine power.

North America (Navajo): the yeii

The many indigenous peoples of North America have animistic gods and goddesses who represent aspects of the natural world and who together make up what is usually called the "Great Spirit" by non-Indians. One of the most complex of Native American deity mythologies is that of the largest American tribe, the Navajo (Dine), who, with their fellow Athabascans, the Apache, arrived in the American Southwest from the north in about 1400 CE. Central to the Navajo pantheon are the yeii, spirit figures, among whom are the Holy People, Talking God, Calling God, Male God, Female God, the hero twins known as Monster Slayer and Born for Water, Shooting God, and many others. These deities figure strongly in Navajo ceremonies and dry (sand) paintings, and they represent important aspects of creation, such as the four directions.

A major deity of the Navajo is Changing Woman (Estsanatlehi), whose movement from young to old and then back to young again stands for the Navajo emphasis on *hozho*, the moral integration that is the goal of the life process and the purpose of the many Navajo rites through which the individual or the tribe moves from disintegration or unwellness to wholeness.

It is said that after beings emerged from the earth, during a period in which monsters prevailed, First Man and First Woman discovered a little turquoise girl, and they raised her. When the child achieved her first menses, First Man and First Woman created a celebratory ceremony for her, the basis for the *kinaalda* ceremony repeated today for Navajo (and Apache) girls when they reach puberty. To begin, First Woman took the role of a deity called Ideal Woman and adorned the girl with jewels. Then she dressed her in a white woven dress and fine moccasins and leggings. In the celebration that followed, the girl became Changing Woman. Each day of the four-day ceremony she ran toward the sun in the east, and each day Ideal Woman massaged her body, conveying to her the strength of womanhood and preparing her later to conceive by the Sun the hero twins, Monster Slayer and Born for Water, who would rid the world of monsters and so provide safety to the people.

One element of the kinaalda ceremony involves the newly pubescent girl baking a corn cake, an act that symbolizes the idea that, as the cake comes from corn and corn from Mother Earth, the girl, like Changing Woman, now has the goddess's changing powers, turning nonlife into life in an ever-continuing cyclical process.

Japan: the kami

The ancient Japanese religion of Shinto is characterized primarily by animist deities known as *kami*. It is sometimes argued that animism is the oldest of religions, preceding organized religions among indigenous peoples in various parts of the world. Animism, from the Latin *anima*, meaning "spirit" or "breath," assumes the existence of spirits in all aspects of life. In this sense, the animistic understanding of life sees no difference between the spiritual world and the physical world. Animism is close to pantheism but differs in that it does not necessarily see the spiritual aspects in all nature as aspects of a unified monistic source such as the Vedantic Brahman.

Animism is particularly present among the indigenous peoples of the Americas and Africa and is sometimes practiced alongside other more organized religions such as Christianity and Islam. Among the Yoruba people of Nigeria and Benin, for instance, *orisha* are spirits that animate all aspects of the earth. In the southwest region of North America, various tribes, including the Hopi, the Zuni, and some of the Tewa and Keres, celebrate figures known as *katsinas* or *kachinas*, embodiments of various elements of nature and human life. There can be kachinas for various ancestors or kachinas representing the sun, the wind, rain, literally any aspect of life. While many of these Native American and African tribes are nominally Christian, ceremonies involving spirits represented by dancers or sculptures are at least as important to the welfare of the tribes as anything that happens in church.

The Japanese kami are the spiritual powers behind all life. Venerated in the Shinto religion ("the Way of the Kami"), the kami emerged from the spiritual realm that existed before creation itself. As described in the sixty-century *Kojiki* ("Records of Ancient Matters") and the eighth-century *Nihongi* ("Japanese Chronicles"), individual kami are associated with the specific aspects of life that they animate. There are an infinite number of kami. These are some of the most important. Amaterasu-Omikami, the sun goddess and ancestress of the Japanese emperors, is "the Great Goddess whose light shines in the Heavens." Among the most ancient is Kami-no-Kaze (Fujin), god of the wind. Yawata-no-Kami (Hachiman) is a god of agriculture and war. Inari Okami is the goddess of fertility. Izanagi and his wife Izanami are the first male and female, whose union gave birth to Japan itself. Ninigi-no-Mikoto (Ninigi), a grandson of Amaterasu, was a direct ancestor of Jimmu, the first Japanese emperor. Tsuki-no-Kami (Tsukiyomi) is the moon god. (Susanowo) is the storm and sea god, the brother and arch rival of Amaterasu.

There are myths told about the kami and their interactions, myths that explain certain realities of existence. It was said, for instance, that Tsukiyomi, the moon god, at one point so angered the sun goddess Amaterasu that she refused ever to look again in his direction. So it is that the sun and moon appear in different parts of the sky. A more famous myth is that of the struggle between Amaterasu and Susanowo. According to the story, one day Susanowo became drunk and belligerent and rushed about heaven, disturbing the peace and causing the destruction of temples dedicated to his sister. In anger and horror, Amaterasu hid in her heavenly cave, thus depriving the world of light and warmth and fertility. As the kami of rice and other plants and animals began to die, the kami captured Susanowo and banished him from heaven. But Amaterasu remained in her cave. Realizing that the world would die without her, the kami devised a plan. They gathered some roosters, which like to crow at dawn. Then they collected an eight-armed mirror and a necklace of beautiful jewels. Next, they instructed the beautiful kami Ame-no-Uzume to dance in a lascivious manner in front of the cave. Eventually, Ama no Azame became so ecstatic that she threw off her clothes and danced naked, causing the kami to laugh so loudly that the roosters began to crow. All of this aroused Amaterasu's curiosity, and she peeked out from the cave to see what was happening. What she saw was her beautiful self reflected in the mirror. As she inched out to see more, warmth and light returned to the world. Amaterasu and Susanowo reconciled and he gave his sister his sword, Kusanagi. Amaterasu gave the sword, the eight-armed mirror, and the necklace of jewels to her grandson Ninigi, the first Japanese emperor. These objects are still used in ceremonies involving the emperor.

Japanese deities, like those of China, serve as metaphysical "explanations" of Japanese history and traditions, particularly those related to the emperor. Some Shinto scholars see the predominance of a goddess, Amaterasu, rather than a male deity, and her reconciliation with the male Susanowo as a necessary masculine/feminine (yin/yang) balance within what is otherwise a highly patriarchal national psyche.

Gods and us

An objective and curious visitor from another planet would inevitably center on the fact that all earthly cultures have deities, sometimes polytheistic, pantheistic, animistic pantheons of gods, in some cases monistic or monotheistic gods. The visitor would also note that, despite some very old traditions—especially in connection with the monotheistic examples—no human had ever seen even one of these deities, but nevertheless, each culture seemed to be sure that its deities, rather than those of other cultures, were the real deities, while deities of other cultures in the past and present were simply the objects of superstitious speculation. Yet people clearly believed their deities to be of sufficient importance to die for them in sometimes brutal and lengthy wars.

Finally, our visitor would have to ask why we humans have gods and goddesses. What do they do for us? Where did they come from? Why are any one culture's deities any more believable or important than those of another? Perhaps divinity exists to establish human identity and cultural significance. In an otherwise hostile or random universe, divine connections provide cultures with a reason for existing. A given culture's gods give that culture particular significance above all others. It is difficult, both as individuals and as cultures, to accept the concept of mere chance existence. So it is that we say we are God's children, or Athena's favorites, or Shaivites, or that Brahman lives within us.

The various perceptions of divinity reflect cultural differences related to such matters as climate, social arrangements, attitudes toward gender, and the concept of sacred royalty or social stratification or hierarchy. Even though we have never seen deities, in one way or another, they are fashioned by us according to our own cultural images of ourselves.

Chapter 2
Creation

Unlike other species, human beings are aware of and constantly fixated on plot—on beginnings, middles, and ends, the past, the present, and the future. We are concerned with personal and family history, but also with the history of the universe and perhaps especially with the history of our own nations or cultures. So it is that all cultures have cosmogonies (kosmos + gonos = universe + offspring), or creation myths. Cosmogonies are etiological—prescientific explanations of the beginning. They explain how the world was created, how given cultures (or humanity as a whole) came into being.

A survey of the mythologies of the world reveals several cosmogony types. In some myths creation is ex nihilo (from nothing), or more precisely, from within the Creator. Creation myths of this type include those in which a god breathes, speaks, or thinks the universe or the world into existence or creates it from its own body. In other myths creation comes from undifferentiated reality or chaos—primordial maternal waters in which earth divers find bits of earth or, for instance, cosmic eggs. Some cultures tell of the creation of the world from the various pieces of a dismembered world parent. Or two world parents are separated so that creation may take place between them. Deus faber (god as maker) myths describe creation in terms of human crafts. For others, people emerged from Mother Earth into an

3. The Creator of the World expels Adam and Eve from the Garden of Eden for their disobedience in this fifteenth-century painting by Giovanni di Paolo di Grazia.

already-created world. What all these types have in common is creation itself. As cultures have needed deities, they have also needed creation myths to establish their own identities.

Egypt: Atum's creation

To consider the creation myth of ancient Egypt is, more precisely, to consider several myths belonging to various cult centers, such as those of Memphis and Heliopolis and Thebes (present-day Luxor and Karnak), some recorded in the Pyramid and Coffin texts. Egyptian creation myths represent many of the familiar creation myth types, including the creation from chaos, the ex nihilo creation, and the world parent creation with its theme of

31

the separation of the parents. The Heliopolis version, for example, answers the mind-teasing question as to what existed before the beginning, that is, before there was a creator or creation. This myth begins with primeval waters, which contain the undifferentiated essential energy or potential necessary for creation. The primeval waters also exist in numerous earth diver myths of the Americas and creation myths of central Asia, Africa, and Polynesia. In the Egyptian myth, the creator god Atum (later Atum-Re) emerged from the waters as the primeval mound, perhaps representing the fertile mounds left annually by the receding waters of the flooded Nile. Atum was the land itself and the rising sun that gave the land light and warmth. Like other creator gods, such as the biblical Yahweh, he was at first alone in the universe and, also like Yahweh, proceeded to create ex nihilo—from himself. In the case of Atum, his mate substitute was his hand (later known as the hand goddess Iusas), with which he masturbated, "that he might obtain the pleasure of emission" and in so doing initiate the creation process. In a later Memphite tradition, Atum swallowed his semen, becoming literally the womb of the "Great He–She." He then, again like Yahweh, thought and named the first elements of his creation. The first born of Atum's mind was the brother–sister couple Shu (Air) and Tefnut (Moisture). In the Coffin texts Atum identifies Shu and Tefnut as Life and Maat (Divine Order). In the Heliopolis myth, Shu and Tefnut, in turn, produced Geb (Earth) and his sister-wife Nut (Sky). Geb and Nut, now the world parents, lay together so closely that they had to be separated by their father Shu, who in so doing, being Air, provided the space between them so that further creation could take place.

The Coffin texts say humans came into existence by way of Shu, who, as Life and Air, breathed life into clay-made objects that became humans. Other myths say that it was Atum who created gods out of his sweat and humans out of his tears. The story has it that Atum lost his eye one day and that Shu and Tefnut found it for him, causing the creator to weep, giving birth to people. From the beginning, then, Egyptian creation mythology places emphasis on creation as birth from waters and other fluids, perhaps mirroring the essential fact of Egyptian survival, the annual flooding of the Nile, and the subsequent resurrection of life in the flood's recession.

Polynesia (Maori): Rangi and Papa

In both the ancient Egyptian and the ancient Greek creations, world parents—maternal Earth and paternal Sky—are locked in so tight an embrace that they must be separated to allow for creation to proceed between them. In the creation myth of ancient Sumer, too, An (Heaven) is separated from Ki (Earth) by the air god Enlil. The Krachi people of Togo and Ghana tell how in the beginning Wulbari (Heaven) lay on Asase Ya (Earth), causing the humans crowded between them to squirm so much that Wulbari had to withdraw from Asase Ya. Similar myths exist in many other parts of the world, including, for instance, in Japan, the ancient continental Celtic lands, and among the Zuni of southwestern North America. Particularly striking examples are found in the mythologies of Polynesia.

The Polynesians, who originated perhaps in Taiwan or elsewhere in East Asia, began their migrations across the South Pacific some 3,500 years ago, settling in Fiji, Tonga, Samoa, Tahiti, New Zealand (Maori), Easter Island, and Hawaii. Among the many Polynesian creation myths, that of the world parents Rangi (Heaven-Sky) and Papa (Earth) stands out.

The Maori, for example, tell how Rangi and Papa were spoken into existence ex nihilo by the words of the creator god Io. Rangi and Papa cleaved together in a coital embrace, leaving little space for their offspring. Some Maori say that while Rangi and Papa were coupling, their children wandered around in the darkness between them but could not see because there was no light. So, the young gods held a council and an angry god, Tumataurenga, argued that the parents must be killed. His brother, Tane-mahutu, the storm god, argued against this plan, as did the agriculture god, Rongo-ma-tane, who stood up, hoping, therefore, to separate the world parents. But his attempt failed, as did that of Tangaroa, the god of oceans, fish, and snakes. It was then that Tane-mahutu stood on his head and pushed his parents apart with his feet. Rangi and Papa cried out in agony at being separated. Rangi's tears fell on Papa, whose sighs rose to her mate as mist. Now, in the new light, people came about and other elements of life, too. But Tangaroa and Tane constantly argued, causing the wind and seas to rage against the people. Tane provided boats, however, so the people could move about the world.

Mesopotamia (Babylon): the *Enuma Elish*

In some mythologies, a single world parent is sacrificed and dismembered, its body parts used to create the world. An early example of this theme exists in a myth told in the city-state of Babylon, one of the Semitic nations that replaced the Sumerian civilization in Mesopotamia. The myth in question is told most fully in an epic known as the *Enuma Elish* ("When on high"), composed or partly compiled from earlier texts—some of them Sumerian—in about 1100 BCE for King Nebuchadnezzar in honor of the Babylonian city god, Marduk.

The epic explains that in the beginning, Apsu, the primordial freshwater, came together with Tiamat, the saltwater. This comingling led to the birth of Lahmu and Lahamni, or land itself. From the union of Lahmu and Lahamni came the gods Anshar and Kishar, who produced the great god Anu (Sumerian An), the sky. It was Anu who fathered the powerful Elil (Sumerian Enlil) and Ea (Sumerian Enki). These younger gods tended to roam about on the ancient waters, the world parents, so disturbing them that Apsu decided to act against them. But Elil and Ea got word of his plans and killed him. Then Ea and the goddess Damkina (Sumerian Ninhursag), the fertility goddess, got together and produced a new god, Marduk, "My son, the Great Sun," as Ea called him.

Meanwhile, furious over the murder of Apsu, Tiamat was also bothered by the waves that constantly bombarded her great body because of the cavorting there of the young gods. So she began to produce monsters to use in a war against them. When the gods failed to subdue Tiamat and her violent minions, young Marduk stepped into the fray. He announced that he would destroy Tiamat and her army if the gods would recognize him as their king. Eventually, the gods agreed, and Marduk, taking up his thunderbolt weapon, stirred up the waters of Tiamat to such a degree that the waters became a gigantic monster, perhaps a dragon. In an ultimate violent act, Marduk prevailed in his struggle with the primordial goddess. He cut her in half, like two pieces of a shellfish, to form a new version of heaven and earth. Out of her body parts he made the paths of the sun and moon. Finally, he had Ea make humans from the bones and blood of Kingu, one of Tiamat's chief monsters, whom he had also killed. The role of these humans was to serve the gods, especially in the city of Babylon where Marduk had his sanctuary.

It seems likely, given the struggle against the waters represented by Apsu and Tiamat and Marduk's close association with Babylon, that Marduk's conquest of Apsu–Tiamat reflects the Babylonian Empire's control of its waterways in the process of fertilizing the land, for agriculture.

Norselands (Iceland): the dismembered Ymir

The Norse creation myth is retold by Snorri Sturluson from the *Voluspa*, a section of the *Poetic Edda*. The myth involves the sacrifice of a single world parent. There was a king of what is now Sweden, who, disguised as an old man named Gangleri, went to Valhalla and met with Odin, who answered his questions about the world and its origins.

Odin told Gangleri that in the beginning there were two places. In the south was Muspell, a place of fire and light. In the north was Niflheim, a place of ice and darkness. The two places met in primeval emptiness between them known as Ginnungagap. The hot and the cold, the light and the dark, mixed there and formed life, beginning with the giant Ymir. Creation was centered by the world tree Yggdrasill. As the world parent, Ymir gave birth to a man and a woman from his armpits and a son from the mating of his two legs. So began the family of frost ogres. Some of the melting ice became the giant cow, Auohumla, out of whose huge teats flowed rivers of milk that fed the first family. The cow licked the ice, eventually revealing a man whose name was Burl, who had a son named Bor, who married Bestla, a daughter of the frost ogres. It was Bor and Bestla who produced the great god Odin as well as the gods Vili and Ve. These three gods proceeded to kill the giant, Ymir. Out of Ymir's remains, the gods made the world. His body became the earth, his blood the seas, his bone the mountains, his teeth the rocks, his skull the sky, and so forth. The three gods then made a new man, Ask, and a woman, Embla, out of two trees, an ash and an elm. Odin breathed life into the new beings, Vi gave them intelligence, and Ve gave them sight and hearing.

The spirit of the sacrifice and dismemberment of Ymir, the world parent, sets the tone for Norse mythology, which is dominated by violent struggles between the various deities, and the death of some, and the apocalyptic dismembering of the world in the horrors of Ragnarok.

Mesoamerica (Aztec): the dismembered goddess

The Aztecs, or, more accurately, the Mexica, were founders of the city of Tenochtitlan, now Mexico City, in about 1350 CE. The Mexica dominated Mesoamerica until their conquest by the Spanish under Cortez in 1521. Aztec mythology owes much to the traditions and deities of the earlier Mesoamerican cultures such as those of the Olmec, the Teotihuacan people, and the Toltec. The god-hero Quetzalcoatl and his rival brother, Tezcatlipoca, for instance, are important to the Mexica mythology but were essentially inherited from the earlier cultures. They play significant roles in one Mexica creation myth, one based on the sacrifice of a world parent, a myth that bears similarities to the creation myths of the Babylonians and the Norse people.

In heaven, Quetzalcoatl (the Feathered Serpent) and Tezcatlipoca watched a huge goddess who floated in the primordial waters below them. The goddess was devouring everything around her, so the two gods decided they must do something about the situation. Turning into giant serpents, they dove into the waters and attacked the goddess, tearing her apart. One part became the earth and the other the sky. The other heavenly gods were upset by the violence of this creative act, so they made certain parts of the dismembered goddess into the beautiful things of our world. Her hair they turned into plants, her eyes water, her shoulders mountains.

It is possible that the dismemberment of the world parent goddess provides mythical justification for the Mesoamerican tradition of human sacrifice. The Mexica, like their predecessors, believed strongly in the concept that, as Mother Earth provides life, she demands payment in lifeblood for that gift.

North America (Penobscot): the sacrifice of Corn Mother

A popular Native American creation figure is the Corn Mother. A goddess who brings corn (maize) to the people, she is typically sacrificed in the process. A story told by the Penobscot tribe of what is now Maine goes like this:

> In the beginning the Creator made a helper from a wave in the primeval maternal waters. One day, as the Creator and his helper were busily creating animals, mountains, plants, and so forth, some dew fell on a plant and was warmed by the sun. Before long the

plant produced a fine young woman. This was First Mother. First Mother mated with the Creator's helper and then gave birth to the people. First Mother taught the people how to live properly, but soon there were too many people, and food was running short. First Mother became sad, and she realized there was only one hope. She told her husband, "You must kill me and then do exactly what I say with my body." Her husband, horrified, refused and went to the Creator for advice. "You must do as she says," said the Creator. So, in great sadness, the husband returned to First Mother and agreed to do what she told him to do.

First Mother said her husband must kill her when the sun was highest in the sky, and then he was to instruct their sons to drag her body over some bare parts of the earth by her long silky hair so that pieces of her body would be scraped off. Then the sons were to go away and only come back after seven moons. When they came back they would find food produced by her sacrificed flesh. And, indeed, when the boys did come back after seven moons, they found that the flesh of First Mother had come to life in the form of beautiful tall plants with long silky hair and a wonderful, delicious and nutritious fruit. So it was that First Mother was now known as Corn Mother. The people saved some of the kernels from the corn each year and buried them in the earth. And, miraculously, each year Corn Mother returned to them as new corn, giving them new life.

Although for many Native Americans the sacrificed Corn Mother would later be assimilated into the myth of the resurrected Jesus, the Corn Mother myth in various forms remains a dynamic reminder to Native Americans of the centrality of corn in their lives and diets. For many, corn is a food charged with the animistic power revealed in the myth of Corn Mother.

India: the Vedic creations

Vedic–Hindu scripture contains many versions of creation. The *Rig-Veda* alone tells several creation myths. One of these builds on the familiar theme of the sacrifice of a world parent. According to the *Veda*, Purusha, a thousand-headed, thousand-footed primal man, contained the universe within himself. A time came when the gods performed a sacrifice of Purusha. His lower quarter became the world. His mouth, the source of words, became the wise Brahmin priest and the god Indra. His arms became the warrior caste, his thighs the common people, and his feet the lowest caste. This sacrifice of Purusha also resulted in animals, plants, rituals, holy words, and the Vedas themselves. From the primal man's mind came the moon, from his eyes the sun, from his breath the wind, from his head the sky, from his feet our earth, and from his navel the air.

India's meditation on creation continued in texts known as the Brahmanas, composed in the first millennium BCE. The *Satapatha Brahmana* contains one of the earliest versions of the cosmic egg motif that would be important in the creation stories of many cultures around the world. The Pelasgians of ancient Greece, for example, believed that the goddess Eurynome laid the egg that hatched the world. Polynesians of Samoa say that the Creator broke out of a cosmic egg and that the broken shells became the Samoan Islands. In Finnish mythology cosmic eggs became earth and sky. The cosmic egg in its many iterations represents the potential for creation—the undifferentiated beginning before the beginning.

The Indian myth begins with the familiar primeval waters. The waters became warm in their strong desire to reproduce, and eventually a golden egg appeared on their surface. After floating about for a time, a first being, Prajapati, emerged from the egg. It took Prajapati almost a year to emerge, much as it takes a woman about that time to produce a child. After he broke out of the egg, Prajapati rested for a long time on the egg's shell. Then he began to create ex nihilo. His breath became sound—the Word—and the word became earth. His next word became the sky. Some of his words became the seasons. Prajapati gave himself the power of reproduction, and he created Agni, the fire god, out of himself. His breath, now hot, rose up into the sky and created light and the gods (*devas*) above. Breathing down, he created darkness, the *asuras*, the dark forces of earth that battle with the gods and their light. Now that there was alternately day and night, light and dark, Prajapati had created time.

In a myth about the creator god Brahma in the Upanishads, texts of the period between 800 and 500 BCE, the cosmic egg was the development of Being from Non-Being. After a year, the egg broke into a silver part and a gold part. The silver part was earth, the gold sky. Inside the egg were the elements of creation—the rivers, the mountains, the plants, the animals. The sun was also born from the egg. The sun was Brahma.

Africa (Dogon): the Nummo

One of the world's most complex cosmic egg myths is that of the Dogon people of the plateau region of what is in the early twenty-first century the African nation of Mali. In the beginning, say the Dogon, there was a maternal world egg. At some point the egg was shaken by seven violent stirrings of the universe, causing it to break into two placentae. Each sac contained a set of twins— one male, one female, but each twin contained the essence of the opposite sex. The egg had been fertilized by the supreme god, Amma (some say the egg was Amma himself). The twins are known as the Nummo. Somehow a male Nummo named Yorugu broke out of a sac early and the broken parts of the sac became the earth. When Yorugu tried to return to the placenta to retrieve his twin sister, she had disappeared. But, in fact, she had been placed somehow in the placenta of the other set of twins. Failing to find his twin, Yorugu went down to the new earth and copulated with it—his own maternal placenta. But no offspring came from this act, so Amma sent the other twins down to procreate, and people were finally born—products of the mating of brother, sister, and cousin twins, all of whom contained both male and female essence.

4. As the result of the mating of Earth and Sky, these divine twins play a central role in the Dogon cosmic egg creation myth. Here they are depicted in a late eighteenth- or early nineteenth-century wood sculpture from southern Mali.

The Nummo myth provides a mythical justification for Dogon marriage rules as well as puberty rituals, the tradition being that the original androgyny of the child is only replaced by adult sexual differentiation when the female element of the penis, the foreskin, and the male aspect of the female organs, the clitoris, are removed.

The Dogon myth, however interpreted, establishes a close connection between the human body and the larger cosmic body of the universe. In that connection humans find an essential significance and sacredness.

China: Pangu and the world egg

A Chinese cosmic egg creation story is a primal man/world parent myth, elements of which resemble both the Indian Purusha and the Dogon Nummo stories. According to the Chinese myth, in the beginning there was only a primordial formless state until that formlessness became an egg. The egg contained the principles yin and yang, universal opposites, which achieved balance. Also in the egg was the giant primal man, Pangu, who after 18,000 years woke up and began the process of creation. He began by separating yin and yang with his axe, forming sky and earth, light and darkness. To maintain the separation between earth and sky, Pangu stood between them, pushing up the sky. With each day, Pangu grew taller, the earth thicker, and the sky higher. After another 18,000 years Pangu died and, like the Norse Ymir and the Babylonian Tiamat, and many other world parents, became the material for further creation. His breath became air and clouds, his left eye the sun, his right eye the moon. His head became the mountains, his muscles land, his blood the waters, his hair the forests.

Another Chinese creation myth originating from the philosophy of Laozi and Daoism emphasizes the Way (Dao) to universal order and understanding. This myth tells us that before there was heaven or earth, there was only the great void. The Dao came from the void as did the cosmos itself. The cosmos gave birth to breath. The yang breath, which was clear light, rose up and became the sky, and the heavier yin breath became the earth.

North America (Iroquois): Sky Woman and the earth divers

For some cultures it was a dive into the primordial waters that led to the creation of the world. Earth diver creation myths are common in central Asia where, for instance, the Altaic, Buriat, and Mongolians all have earth diver myths. This type of myth is even more ubiquitous among the Algonquian and Iroquoian-speaking tribes of North America. Particularly elaborate versions of the theme are those of the Iroquois Federation in what is now New York State. This is a Seneca story, told with minor variations by each of the six Iroquoian tribes.

There was a time long ago when there was no world, no earth, only water everywhere and a few ducks, other water birds, a turtle, and a toad floating on it. What people there were lived in a place in the sky with the Great Chief. The Chief had a daughter, and one day the daughter fell sick and seemed about to die. In a dream, a wise man learned that the girl needed to be placed next to a certain tree and that the tree should then be dug up. The Chief accepted the truth of the dream and had his daughter placed next to the tree, which he then had dug up. Then another man came along and pushed the girl into the hole left by the digging, and the girl fell through the hole into space. As she was floating down towards the great water, the water birds there saw her coming and with their wings they formed a soft landing place for her. When the birds got tired of holding the girl, they placed her on the turtle's back. But after a time, the turtle got tired too, so the birds asked the toad to dive into the waters for some soil so that a firmer living place could be made for the girl. The toad succeeded in finding some soil in the depths, brought it up to the surface, and placed it on the turtle's back. It should be said here that many tribes say that several small animals tried and lost their lives trying to accomplish this task. Most say it was the lowly muskrat who finally succeeded. In any case, the soil on the turtle's shell began to grow, and the shell grew too. Soon there was the earth for the girl—Sky Woman, as she was called—to live on (some call Earth Turtle Island), and she was happy there in a little house. Then one day she gave birth to a little girl. The mother and daughter worked the land for food, and before long the daughter produced twins.

One of the twins was named Othagwenda (Flint), the other Juskaha (Sapling). But Sky Woman disliked Othagwenda, so she placed him in a tree, and she taught Juskaha how to make things and hunt. But Juskaha was meeting up secretly with his brother, and one day he brought him home. For a while things went well enough, and the twins enlarged the earth. But then Othagwenda began doing bad things. He created bad land that could not be worked, and he created Mosquito, an insect so huge it could cut down trees. Juskaha was horrified by Mosquito, fearing for the people he planned to create. So he rubbed the insect down to his present size. And he made good things, like animals and edible plants. But Othagwenda continued making problems for the new people and other things his brother had created. So eventually the twins fought, and Juskaha killed Othagwenda. But it was too late to get rid of the bad things the bad twin had left behind.

The Iroquoian earth diver myth with its emphasis on Sky Woman and her daughter reflects the matrilineal traditions of the Iroquois. The conflict between the twins represents a realistic view of life on earth.

The twin motif is a constant one in world mythology. The bad twin here takes the place of a devil figure who interferes with the Creator's work in many central Asian earth diver creation myths, a figure related to the trickster.

North America (Acoma): the emergence from the earth

A creation myth type, one that is prevalent in the southwestern part of North America among the Pueblos along the Rio Grande and the Acoma, Laguna, Zuni, Hopi, and Navajo further west, is the emergence myth. Like the earth diver creation, the emergence pattern emphasizes the centrality of the sacred earth. In it, the people are born of the earth as a symbolic mother, often assisted by specific goddess figures. The significant female is in keeping with the matrilineal kinship systems of many of the southwestern tribes. Versions of the myth are told in *kivas*, structures that themselves are architectural representations of the birth motif. For ceremonial dances, the participants emerge from a hole in the roof of many of the kivas and on the kiva floor is a small hole, the *sipapu*, indicating the place of the tribes' emergence from Mother Earth. The version of the emergence myth below is one told by the Acoma people, whose ancient village sits on top of a mesa in the western region of what is now New Mexico.

In the beginning, the dark underground gave birth to twin sister-spirits. The sisters were fed by a goddess, Tsichtinako (Thinking Woman), who also taught them speech. When Tsichtinako thought the sisters were ready for creation, she gave them baskets that contained seeds for all the plants that would grow in the upper world and models for all the animals that would live there. The goddess helped the twins to find the seeds for four trees that she said should be planted in the darkness before the emergence into the light of the upper world. After a long time, one of the trees—the pine—grew sufficiently to break a small hole in the earth above, letting in some light. With more help from Tsichtinako, the girls found in one of their baskets the model of the badger, to whom they gave life. They instructed the badger to dig around the hole above to make it a bit larger. They warned the badger not to enter the upper world, however. The badger followed their instructions, so they awarded him a promise of eventual happiness in the world above. Next the twins found the model for the locust, and after giving him life, they asked him to smooth the opening above, warning him not to stray into the upper world. After smoothing out the hole, the locust returned but admitted that he had passed through it briefly. The girls scolded him and said that as a punishment he would have to live underground and die each year once they emerged into the upper world.

Now it was time to emerge, so, instructed by Tsichtinako, the sisters took their baskets, climbed the pine tree up to the hole, and broke through into the upper world. There they waited for the light they had been told would arise in the east. When the light came, they sang the song of creation for the first time. Tsichtinako revealed to the girls, now named Iatiku (Life-Bringer) and Nautsiti (Full Basket), that their father, Uchtsiti, had made the upper world from a clot of his blood and that they were to complete the creation by planting their seeds of life.

Australia (Yolugu): a Dreamtime walkabout

A unique creation type is that of many Aboriginal people of Australia. Creation for these people took place in what is usually translated as the "Dreamtime," a kind of mythological age during which primordial beings did walkabouts that left sacred markings and objects and established taboos, rituals, and other societal structures. It was during "the Dreaming" that people were created. Myths describing the Dreamtime vary from tribe to tribe. A myth involving Dreamtime beings known as the Djanggawul is told by the Yolugu of Eastern Arnheim Land.

In the beginning, certain prehuman ancestors existed. These were Djanggawul and his two sisters, Bildjiwraroiju and Miralaidj. The three traveled about in their bark canoe in the Dreamtime to places they wanted to populate. Djanggawul and his sisters had unusually large sexual organs. Djanggawul's organ was decorated with notches. Wherever they beached their canoe they left offspring fathered by Djanggawul on his two sisters. To mate successfully, Djanggawul had to lift the oversized sex organs of his mates. When the three walked about on land, their sex organs dragged along the ground, leaving sacred markings, or "dreamings," some of which still exist in the early twenty-first century. They also left certain ceremonies. In many of these, their sex organs, represented by decorated poles, were central objects of devotion. They also left stories as they went, and they created many other things from their sacred thoughts.

When Djanggawul and his sisters came to their final destination in Arnheim Land, they camped in the waterhole there that was made when they inserted one of their sacred phallic poles into the ground. A sacred spring still flows from the spot. Some say that when they arrived in Arnheim they instituted the practice of male and female circumcision to overcome the inconvenience of their exaggerated genital parts.

Creation and us

These creation myths particularize universal themes. As such, they wear a wide variety of cultural clothes, revealing a sense of how ultimate reality takes form in particular cultural environments. We tell creation stories to establish ourselves meaningfully in the center of the world in which we happen to find ourselves. Our creation myths remind us of who we are, as particular cultures, bringing the childhood of our cultural and spiritual history into our present experience. Creation myths are our bridges to the divine world of the deities. It is creation myths that establish our significance in a world that would otherwise seem to be random and arbitrary.

Chapter 3
The flood

Flood myths are found in literally all corners of the world. They exist in places like Egypt and Mesopotamia, where floods are an aspect of actual experience, as well as in places where they are not. In most cases, the flood, or great deluge, is brought about by a creator deity or deities displeased with the way humans have managed themselves and the created world. In many cases, the flood myth features a worthy individual who, acting as a culture hero, provides a means by which the world can be re-created.

Mesopotamia (Sumer/Babylon): Utnapishtim

The oldest known flood myth is that of Mesopotamia. The myth is told in the context of the epic story of the hero Gilgamesh. Remnants of the Gilgamesh story and the flood myth exist on ancient Sumerian tablets, dating from as early as 2100 BCE. Much fuller versions are attributed to the Semitic rulers of Mesopotamian who followed in the wake of the Sumerians. An Akkadian version was compiled in about 1800 BCE, and the so-called Standard Babylonian version, generally known as the *Epic of Gilgamesh*, was completed in about 1100 BCE. One of the Sumerian tablets tells how the gods, while at a drunken banquet, created humans to serve them. These humans proved to be weak and problematic, and, eventually, the gods decided to do away with them in a great flood. The Gilgamesh epic explains that one man, Utnapishtim (Ziusudra in the Sumerian original, Atrahasis in the Akkadian version), his family, and a few other people survived in a boat.

The epic tells the story of Gilgamesh's quest for eternal life, which takes him to the flood hero. Utnapishtim explains that Enlil, having decided to destroy his human creation in a flood, decided to spare him. He was to take his family, a few other willing people, and samples of all living things into a boat. The boat was to be constructed according to the god's instructions. It was a large, cube-like vessel with nine rooms in each of seven levels.

5. This ancient cuneiform tablet, dating from the seventh or sixth century BCE, tells part of the Mesopotamian flood myth as related in the many versions of the Gilgamesh story.

Utnapishtim, as instructed, loaded it with food, wine, and the seeds of all living beings. Then Ea (the Sumerian Enki) sent rains that covered the earth in water. On the seventh day of the flood, the ship hit Mount Nisir. Utnapishtim sent out birds—the dove, the swallow, and the raven—to see if there was any dry land. The dove and the swallow returned, indicating that there was still no dry land. When the raven did not come back, Utnapishtim realized there was now dry land, so he had the people leave the ship. He, however, waited for Enlil to come to him with further instructions. Enlil came to Utnapishtim and blessed him, saying he and his wife would be treated like gods now, with eternal life, and would live at the source of what were later called the Tigris and Euphrates Rivers. The goddess Ishtar (Sumerian Inanna) declared that such a flood would never occur again and presented her lapis lazuli necklace as a sign of that promise.

Israel: Noah

It has long been noted that there are similarities between the Mesopotamian myth and the biblical myth of Noah and the ark. The final version of the Babylonian *Epic of Gilgamesh*—the fullest version of the Mesopotamian myth—was written down perhaps as late as about 700 BCE. The biblical story of Noah was written in the sixth century BCE during the period of the Babylonian exile, the captivity of Israelites in Babylon. That there would have been a Babylonian influence on the biblical story would not, therefore, be surprising.

According to the Bible (and the Quran), God became fed up with the wickedness of humans and decided to wipe them off the face of the earth in a flood. But Noah (Nu in Arabic) was a righteous man. And God decided to save him, his wife, their three sons, and the sons' wives. He told Noah to build an ark of cypress wood, three hundred cubits long, fifty wide, and thirty high, with three decks, several rooms, and a roof and a side door. Noah was then to bring into the ark seven pairs of all living things, as well as his family. Then the rains came and kept coming for forty days, covering even the highest mountains. Everything and everyone outside the ark perished. Finally, God sent a wind, which pushed aside the waters, and after many days, the ark landed on Mount Ararat. After a time, Noah opened a window and sent out a raven and then a dove to see if there was dry land. The raven flew about, its wings helping to dry the land, and on its second flight the dove returned with a leaf. After another week Noah sent out the dove again, and it did not return. So Noah knew that the land was now dry. God told him to open the side door of the ark and to come out with all the animals. Noah did so, and he built an altar and made sacrifices on it. God was pleased and vowed never again to destroy the world with a flood. As a sign of this covenant, he placed a rainbow in the sky. As for Noah, he lived to be 950 years old.

Africa (Masai): Tumbainot

This Masai myth resembles those of Sumer and the Bible and is almost certainly an example of the influence of colonial religion on the colonialized.

A good man named Tumbainot and his wife Naipande had three sons. After the death of his brother, Tumbainot, according to custom, married his brother's widow, Nahaba-logunja. She, in turn, gave birth to three sons. There were too many people in the world at the time, and the people had become evil and neglectful of God. So, God decided to destroy the world in a flood. Only Tumbainot and his family were to be saved. God ordered Tumbainot to build an ark for himself and his family and samples of the animals and plants of the earth. Then the rains came and flooded the earth. After a long time, Tumbainot sent out a dove from the ark to find out if there was dry land. The exhausted dove returned, having found no land. Sometime later, Tumbainot sent out a vulture with an arrow in its feathers. Tumbainot believed that if there was dry land, the arrow would become attached to something and the vulture would return, proving that there was dry land. As planned, the vulture returned without the arrow, so Tumbainot knew the flood was receding. In time, the ark landed on dry land and the people and animals entered a new world. God sent four rainbows to celebrate the end of the flood.

Greece and Rome: Deucalion and Pyrrha

The Noah and the Utnapishtim myths have close mythical relatives in various parts of the world, including Greece and Rome. Ancient Greek flood myths are referred to by Hesiod, Plato, and others. An elaborate retelling and embellishment of the Greek myth is that of the Roman poet Ovid in his 8 BCE work the *Metamorphoses*.

According to Ovid, Jupiter (Zeus) descends to earth to see for himself what he has heard are the evil ways of human beings. He visits the home of a man named Lycaon, who prepares a feast for the god. But the feast is a sham. Lycaon plans to murder Jupiter and serves him human flesh in the meal. Furious, Jupiter sees Lycaon as an example of evil humanity. He returns to Olympus and announces his intention of obliterating the entire human race. He begins by sending a thunderbolt to destroy Lycaon's house. Then he turns Lycaon into a wolf and prepares to inundate the world in a great flood. Meanwhile, the Titan Prometheus warns his pious son Deucalion of the coming flood and prepares a boat for him and his good wife, Pyrrha, a daughter of Pandora, of Pandora's box fame, to ride out the deluge.

Using the waters of the sky and those of the sea, Jupiter floods the earth, destroying humanity and all other living things except for Deucalion and Pyrrha, who survive in their boat for nine days before landing on Mount Parnassus when the flood waters begin to recede. They go to the Temple of Themis, the Titan "Goddess of Good Counsel," to ask for help in restoring the human race. Themis tells them they must leave her temple with their heads veiled and that they must throw the "bones" of their mother behind them. Eventually Deucalion and Pyrrha realize that by bones of the mother, Themis meant stones of Mother Earth. When the couple threw down stones, the stones became new humans. When Deucalion and Pyrrha settled finally in Thessaly, they produced two sons who became the fathers of the Dorians, the Ionians, the Aeolians, and the Achaeans—the tribes of the ancient Greeks.

Mesoamerica (Aztec): Tata and Nena

The Aztec (Mexica) flood myth resembles others around the world. According to their myth, the people of a certain stage of creation became unruly and gave up proper worshiping of the gods. This angered the gods, and the rain god Tlaloc decided to flood the earth to destroy its human inhabitants. Only a good couple, Tata and his wife, Nena, were to be spared. Tlaloc warned the couple of the imminent flood and told them they could find safety by hollowing out a log and getting into it. Tata and Nena were to take only two ears of corn to sustain them through the deluge, and they were to eat nothing else until Tlaloc gave them further instructions. The good couple did as they were instructed until the flood subsided and they landed on dry ground. But then they disobeyed the god by catching and eating a fish. Furious, Tlaloc turned the couple into dogs before creating a new world.

South America (Inca): the making of Lake Titicaca

The Inca of South America have several flood myths. Some say that the god Viracocha created a world with giants to live in it. But the giants quickly became ungrateful and violent—so much so that the Creator decided they must be destroyed. He turned some of the giants into stone statues that still exist in various places. The rest he destroyed in a great flood—all except two giants who helped him make normal-sized humans to repopulate the earth.

Another Incan flood story concerns a rich city named Altiplano. Some poor Indians came one day to that city and warned the people there that a flood would soon destroy the city. The people made fun of the Indians and threw them out of the city. But some of the city's priests believed the flood warning and moved to a temple on a mountaintop. Soon a huge red cloud appeared in the sky, an earthquake destroyed the city's buildings, and a red rain poured down. Other earthquakes and more rain followed, and a flood soon covered the ruined city. This water is Lake Titicaca today.

Pictorial records of ancient Incan rulers show that a flood rose above the highest mountains. All created things perished, except for a man and woman who floated in a box. When the flood subsided, the floating box was driven by the wind to Tiahuanacu. There the Creator molded new people from clay. He gave each figure a certain hair and clothes style as well as a particular language. He made the people go underground before emerging into the new existence. Finally, he created the sun, moon, and stars for this new world of many nations.

North America (Hopi): Spider Woman and the flood

Some Hopi people of the American Southwest also combine a flood myth with an emergence in one of many versions of their creation. They say that while the people were still living underground within Mother Earth, they began to undermine the Creator's laws with their arrogance and disruptiveness. So the Creator decided to destroy that world. First, he sent fire and then cold to destroy the evil people. Some good people survived underground, and the Creator called on Spider Woman to help these people. She protected the good people by placing them in giant reeds. Then, when the Creator sent a great flood to finish off the remaining bad people, the good people floated up to the top of the water in their reeds. When the reeds came to rest on a piece of dry land, the people emerged and made their way in canoes to the world they live in now.

Thailand: the gourd

In a Thai flood myth somewhat similar to that of the Hopi, a gourd plays the part of the Hopi reeds. According to the myth, the Creator, Phu Ruthus, created First Man (Sangkasa) and First Woman (Sangkasi), who in turn produced many children. Then their children produced children, until about 1,000 years had passed. Unfortunately, the descendants of the first couple gradually forgot to worship the Creator and became unruly. Angry at this situation, the Creator decided to clean out the world in a great flood. A few people managed to survive the flood by hiding in a giant gourd. After a time, the Creator decided to allow these people to live. He sent two lesser gods down from heaven to the gourd by way of a vine. Once arriving at the gourd, these gods released the humans preserved there and led them to a new land that existed above the receding flood waters. Once there, the two gods acted as culture heroes, teaching the people how to survive.

Egypt: the beer flood

The Egyptian flood myth is a late third-millennium BCE story that resembles the many myths containing the theme of an evil humanity punished by the supreme deity. It differs radically in its treatment of the flood itself and the means by which humanity is eventually saved.

The myth begins with a corrupt humanity plotting against the great sun god Re (Atum-Re, Amun-Re), causing the god to call a council of the gods who had been with him in the primeval waters at the time of creation. The council included Nun, who was the god of watery chaos, as well as Re's "eye," the goddess Hathor. Nun advised Re that the rebellious humans—the children of his eye— be punished by the eye. All the gods agreed, so Hathor, assisted by another aspect of Re's eye, the violent lion goddess Sekhmet—perhaps the sun—descended to the humans in the desert below, killing almost all of them until Re intervened. Taking pity on his creation, he made beer out of barley and red ochre and flooded the fields of Egypt with it. The beer appealed to Hathor, and she drank so much of it that she became drunk and forgot about slaughtering humans.

Like so many Egyptian myths, this one is likely to have its source in the annual destructive but beneficial flooding of the Nile.

India: Manu and the fish

The flood plays an important role in the mythology of India. Several ancient texts dating from the eighth to the sixth centuries BCE, including the *Vishnu Purana* and the *Satapatha Brahmana*, the later *Matsya Purana*, and the epic poem the *Mahabharata*, all contain variations of a flood myth in which the flood hero is the first man, Manu. The myth begins with a simple daily act. Manu (or, according to some texts, the king of Dravadia) was washing his hands in the morning when he noticed a little fish in his hands. The fish spoke to him, saying, "Take care of me, and I will save you." When Manu asked how he was to be saved and from what, the fish revealed that there would be a great flood from which he would save Manu. "But how can I take care of you in the meantime?" asked Manu. The fish instructed Manu to put him in a jar while he was still small, and later, when he was bigger, in a small pond. Finally, when he was big enough, the fish was to be placed in the sea. After all this was done, the fish, now huge, revealed himself to be Matsya, the fish avatar (incarnation) of the great god Vishnu. Matsya informed Manu of the coming of the deluge and told him how to build a ship that would save him, his family, and various animals and seeds that would be needed to begin a new world. The flood occurred as predicted, and Manu's ship was saved by means of a rope tied to the horn on Matsya's head and later to a tree on the Malaya Mountains. As the water

6. This late nineteenth-century painting depicts the giant fish Matsya, one of the ten avatars of the god Vishnu, as he saves the world from a great flood.

gradually receded, Manu allowed the ship to slowly descend to the drying earth below. Thus, he and the ship's contents were saved, and a new cycle of existence could begin. This all took place several million years ago.

Mesoamerica (Maya): Huracan's flood

According to the Mayan text known as the *Popol Vuh* (The book of the people), the storm god Huracan (the "One-legged One"), whose name is the source of the modern word *hurricane*, was responsible for an ancient world-destroying flood. The flood story here is intricately involved in the creation of the current race of human beings. The Mayan creation myth explains that the gods first created mountains and plants, but they wanted sound, so they created animals. But the animals were unable to express themselves or to properly worship the gods, so the gods decided to create humans to oversee the animals. Huracan and the god known as the Plumed Serpent experimented with human creation. First they tried people made of mud. But these people simply fell apart. Next they tried making people of wood. These people could talk, but they had difficulty moving, could not remember anything, and could not worship the gods. Furious with these wooden people, Huracan sent a flood to destroy them. After days of continuous rain, all that was left of the wood people were monkeys.

After a while, Huracan called out "Earth," and land arose from the mist above the flood. Later, real people would emerge from three men and four women left to repopulate the world after the flood.

The Mayan flood myth is unique in that the flood is sent by the gods not so much to punish human corruption as to make up for a mistake made by the gods themselves in the creative process.

China: Yu, the flood tamer

One of the most complex and original flood myths is the Chinese story of Yu, found in the *Shu Ching* (Book of documents), the compiling of which has been attributed to Confucius (551–479 BCE). The myth itself dates to perhaps as early as 1000 BCE. As is the case with much of Chinese mythology, the story is associated with ancient semidivine emperors, who straddle the line between history and legend.

It is said that during the reign of the emperor Yao, a great flood covered the land and even threatened heaven itself. The high god asked Gun (Kun) to control the flood, but his nine years of labor against it failed, and he was executed. Gun's son Yu, later known as Yu the Great (2123–2025 BCE), was ordered to take up the task. For thirteen years Yu devoted himself to his mission, not even visiting his home. His determination and dedication earned him the respect of the people and made him a symbol of these characteristics for later generations.

Yu used practical and worldly strategies against the deluge. His father had used soil-based dikes against the waters, but they had failed. Instead of simply blocking the waters, Yu made channels and barricades to lure the waters away from the land into the sea.

There are many legends surrounding Yu and the flood. Some tell how the Yinglong (Responding Dragon) helped by using his giant tail to channel the water. Another story says that He Bo, the god of the Yellow River, gave Yu a map to help him direct the waters. In the struggle against the flood, Yu overcame several monsters that threatened human life. Xiang Liu, a nine-headed monster, turned land into marshes and gullies in which nothing could survive. Yu executed this monster. Another monster was Wuzhiqi, who lived in the Huai River and, with his followers, caused storms that interfered with Yu's work. So Yu enlisted the help of the gods, including many who had formerly supported Wuzhiqi, to control the monster. It was a being known as Gengchen who finally defeated Wuzhiqi and brought the Huai River under control for Yu.

Stories tell how Yu married a woman from Tushan. In some versions of the myth, Yu left his wife after the fifth day of their marriage and went back to work controlling the flood. Other texts say that Yu's wife helped him in his work. In one story, Yu was busily excavating through a mountain to channel water to the sea when he decided to change himself into a bear. He told his wife to bring him food whenever she heard the sound of his drum. By mistake, Yu—in his form as a bear—stepped on his drum, and his wife came immediately with food. Horrified at finding her husband changed to a bear, she fled the tunnel and then began to turn into a stone just as she was about to give birth. When Yu found his wife—now a rock—he called for his son, who broke out of a split in the rock. This son, Qi, later inherited his father's power and became emperor of China. After the thirteen years of Yu's work to redirect the waters in such a way as to end the great deluge, the world became dry again so that people could settle on it and cultivate the land.

As the primary figure in the flood myth, Yu is a much more active hero figure than other figures such as Noah, Utnapishtim, and Manu. In great part this is because of the Chinese tendency to relate myth to actual history and to practical rather than theological matters. The story of Yu is a metaphor for the process of water control and irrigation that made an agricultural civilization possible in ancient China.

Celtic (Ireland): Cessair

Another culture in which flood mythology is tied to history is that of Celtic Ireland. The *Lebor Gabala* (The book of invasions) and other monastic texts tell of several invasions that were thought to make up Irish history and civilization from the beginnings to the Middle Ages. The invaders include the people of Cessair, the people of Partholón, the people of Nemed, strange beings known as the Fir Bolg, a race of gods, the Tuatha De Danann, and finally, the Milesians.

The tale of the first invaders, the people of Cessair, contains the remnants of a flood myth that is influenced by biblical narratives. Cessair was a granddaughter of the biblical flood hero, Noah. In some versions of the Cessair myth, Noah tells Cessair's people to flee to the edge of the world to escape the coming flood. In another version, Cessair and her people are denied a place in Noah's ark, so Cessair instructs her people to follow the advice of an idol, who tells them to make their way to Ireland to escape the flood. Sailing in three ships, the Cessair party arrived in Ireland, where two of the ships were wrecked. Only Cessair, forty-nine other women, and three men, Fintan, Bith, and Ladra, survived. According to the myth, the party landed in Ireland forty days before Noah's flood, in 2242 BCE. Others say it was 2361 BCE. The men shared the women, but eventually everyone but Fintan died. He fled to a cave in the mountains, and when the flood finally arrived in Ireland, he turned himself into a one-eyed salmon, then into an eagle, and then a hawk to survive. After 5,500 years, he became a man again and told the tale of the flood. As for Cessair, her body is said to have been buried in County Roscommon.

Norselands (Iceland): Ymir's blood

The Norse people, neighbors of the Celts, told a different sort of flood myth, but one with echoes of the most ancient of such myths. The *Poetic Edda* explains that when the gods killed the giant Ymir, so much blood flowed from his body that all the frost giants but one drowned in it. Only the giant Bergelmer and his wife survived by boarding an ark of sorts and riding out the deluge.

The flood and us

A theme that finds its way into many aspects of world mythology is that of the productive sacrifice. Flood myths are convenient vehicles for this theme. They involve a universal death that leads to an equally universal rebirth. The flood is, above all, a cleansing act, one that provides a second creation, a second chance for humanity. The old life is swept away, but the germ of a new life survives in the flood hero's ark. That the new creation is preceded by a devastating flood is appropriate since life in most creation myths emerged originally from the primordial maternal waters. In this sense, rituals of purification by water, whether Jewish *mikvahs* or Muslim preprayer ablutions or Japanese *misogi* bathing, for example, are microcosmic versions of the flood. Baptism is an especially clear example. In the Christian baptismal rite, the "sinner" is immersed in the waters of the font and in the process "dies" to the old life before emerging, "born" to a new life. The flood hero, then, locked in the ark of survival, represents a universal hope for a new beginning.

Chapter 4
The trickster

The trickster is a complex and contradictory character who appears in many guises in world mythology, often in connection with creation myths. He is both creative and destructive, a selfish thief and sometimes a culture hero who teaches his people. He is immoral, or at least amoral. He has insatiable appetites. Although powerful, he can be the foolish butt of his own tricks. He can change shapes at will, often taking the form of his totem animal.

Mesopotamia (Sumer): Enki

Among the most important of Sumerian gods in ancient Mesopotamia was Enki, who became Ea later in Babylon. While not exactly a trickster, Enki (Lord of the Earth) had several trickster attributes. He is associated with two animals, the goat and the fish, both symbols of fertility in Sumer. Enki's personal symbol was a combination of the two animals as the goat-fish. And Enki was nothing if not fertile. Life-giving water in Sumer was Enki's semen. Like tricksters in later traditions, Enki had an insatiable sexual appetite. This characteristic stands out in the tale of Enki and his consort, the Mother Goddess Ninhursaga.

Enki and Ninhursaga produced a daughter, Ninsar, with whom Enki had sex that produced Ninkurra, with whom he also had intercourse, leading to the birth of Uttu. When Enki approached

Uttu for sex, Ninhursaga intervened. But in some versions of the tale, the intercourse takes place, and Ninhursaga takes the semen from the girl's womb and places it in the earth, which gives birth to fruit-bearing plants.

The deeds of tricksters often lead to tricks being played on the trickster himself. In this case, Enki, who also had a strong appetite for food, ate the fruit of the new plants. Having eaten the produce of his own semen, he becomes pregnant. But because he is male and has no means of giving birth, he writhes in agony until Ninhursaga relents and allows him to inject his water (semen) into her body. It is important to note that in Sumer sexuality— even incestuous sexuality as in the somewhat comic Enki– Ninhursaga tale—ultimately provided metaphors for the fertility of the land rather than for moral standards such as those a modern audience might apply to Enki's incestuous acts. In the myth in question, for instance, the "violated" Ninkurra and Ninsar are "Lady of Pastures" and "Lady Greenery," respectively.

Enki, like the tricksters of many later cultures, was a crafty magician. According to a Sumerian myth, *Enmerkar and the Lord of Aratta*, it was he, for instance, who changed languages so that instead of speaking one, the people of the world spoke many.

A myth concerning a visit to Enki in the city of Eridu by the great goddess Inanna reveals more trickster aspects. The myth describes how Enki plies himself and his visitor with beer and fails in an attempt to seduce her. His deeds come back to haunt him when, in his drunken state, he gives up his control of the *me*—the divine foundations of civilized Sumerian life and institutions—to the goddess. Hungover the next morning, Enki discovers what he has done and attempts but fails to retrieve the *me*, which Inanna takes to her home city, Uruk.

Like other tricksters, Enki can also use his magic and skills as a de facto culture hero who serves the best interests of humanity by circumventing the will of other gods. In the flood myths of Mesopotamia, it is Enki who defies the head god Enlil (Elil) by devising the ark for Utnapishtim (Ziusudra, Atrahasis) and, in one version of the myth, by teaching the flood hero secrets of irrigation, medicine, and other means of survival. It was also Enki who used his cunning to free Inanna from the clutches of her sister Ereshkigal in the underworld, thus preserving the stability and fertility of Sumer.

Egypt: Set

In nearby Egypt, another figure with strong trickster characteristics played a major role in a struggle against the holy family of Osiris, Isis, and their son Horus. This figure was Set (Seth). Like trickster-type characters elsewhere, Set was a shapeshifter who could take any number of animal forms. Though at some periods and places in Egypt he was a powerful and positive figure, in the Osiris saga his ambiguity made him a god of confusion rather than a supporter of *maat*, roughly the Egyptian equivalent of the Sumerian *me*—the sacred elements of justice, civilization, and order.

Set is said to have left the womb of his mother, Nut (Sky), violently, to have turned against his sister-wife Nephthys, and later to have murdered his brother Osiris, the god-king of Egypt, in effect a culture hero who, accompanied by his sister-wife Isis, taught the Egyptians how to live by laws, how to grow crops, and how to worship the gods. The Set–Osiris conflict is central to the whole Egyptian concept of fertility, resurrection, and the afterlife.

Set's disruptive but creative trickery did not end with his attacks on Osiris. He continued to try to undermine his young nephew Horus, who was born of Isis in the Egyptian delta. In so doing he made use of the creative but antisocial (or, in this case, anti-*maat*) powers and the sexual proclivities of the universal trickster.

The *Kahun Papyri* of the Middle Kingdom reports that Set became so jealous of his popular young nephew that he decided to rid himself of him by any means possible. When various tricks failed, he decided that his best approach would be to humiliate Horus sexually before the gods by labeling him a passive homosexual. He invited his teenaged nephew to a party, plied him with liquor, convinced him to stay the night in his bed, and raped him in his apparent sleep. But Horus, who had only pretended to be drunk, prevented Set's semen from entering him. He told his mother, Isis, what had happened, and she instructed the boy to take some of his own semen and rub it on the leaves of Set's favorite food, a kind of lettuce grown only in Egypt. Set ate the lettuce before going to the gods to report that he had sexually penetrated Horus. The gods ordered that, as proof, Set's semen be extracted from Horus. When no semen was found, the boy suggested that, in fact it was *his* semen which was in *Set*. When Horus's semen was extracted from Set, who had eaten Horus's semen-treated lettuce, it was Set rather than Horus who was humiliated. Like so many tricksters, Set became the butt of his own tricks.

The Horus–Set sexual contest reveals an ancient Egyptian belief, shared by many cultures, that only the receiver of semen, in effect, playing the female role in intercourse between males, is a homosexual, the penetrator having performed what was seen as a masculine act.

Israel: the serpent

Satan has trickster characteristics, particularly in the Christian interpretation of the Hebrew Bible's (Old Testament) book of Genesis. In the first of the two human creation stories told in the book (Gen. 1:26–28), Yahweh (God) creates an unnamed man and woman in his own image, gives them dominion over the earth, and orders them to be fruitful and multiply. In Genesis 2 the Bible tells a slightly different story. Here, God creates a man, later called

Adam, out of dust and breathes life into him. In time, he made a female companion for Adam. He did this by putting the man to sleep and making a woman out of one of the man's ribs. "Woman" was so named because she was created from the man. Adam and the woman were naked, but not ashamed.

In Genesis 2 God had created the Garden of Eden for Adam, instructing him to eat anything in it except for one tree. This tree was the Tree of the Knowledge of Good and Evil. To eat from it would bring death into the world.

The woman created out of Adam was tempted one day by a being identified simply as the serpent (*nahash*). This serpent is typically seen by Christians as a personification of the fallen angel Satan. For Jews, *satan* refers not to a particular being but simply to negative forces that threaten humans. For Muslims, *shayatin* is something between these two understandings. It is the Christian interpretation that has achieved dominance in the collective popular mind. This interpretation owes much to the archetype of the trickster. Like other tricksters, Satan takes an animal form. He is subtle and clever in his arguments, as he convinces Eve to eat fruit from the forbidden tree. Eat from the tree, he argues, and you will be able to understand good and evil and thus be on an equal plane with gods. Eve eats from the tree and convinces Adam to do so too. Like other tricksters, then, Satan undermines the Creator's work. As in other trickster tales, this undermining takes the form of the introduction of pain and, especially, death into creation. As for the perpetrator, he is turned into the serpent more familiar to us, the slithering and potentially poisonous snake who is feared as a potential threat. As is often the case, the trickster pays for his antisocial deeds.

Satan in Genesis indirectly passes on to the first humans the concept of uncontrolled sexuality usually associated with tricksters. After eating the fruit of the forbidden tree, Adam and Eve suddenly become aware of their nakedness and cover their genitals with leaves. Natural sexuality becomes shameful sex. With their new knowledge, the couple is expelled from the garden and forced to live in what we would call real life.

It must be remembered that tricksters nearly always have a creative and positive side, frequently working in support of humans in an imperfect world. In this sense, for instance, the Greek Titan Prometheus, who steals fire from the gods to benefit humans, can be considered a positive trickster. The biblical trickster has sometime been seen in the more positive light of the so-called fortunate fall. In one complex Christian theological understanding, for instance, Adam and Eve's sin was the source of redemption in the person of Jesus. In this argument, Satan did cause Adam and Eve to eat of the Tree of the Knowledge of Good and Evil, but in so doing he opened the way to a new tree of life, the cross, on which the new fruit, Jesus, hung and overcame death itself.

Central Asia (Buryat): the Creator's "helper"

A devil/trickster as an undermining influence plays a significant role in most central Asian creation myths. In a pre-Islamic Turkic myth he is Er-Kishi, who interferes with Tengri's creation. In a Tungus myth from Manchuria, the devil Buninka tried to "help" the Creator in his work but only succeeded in weakening it. In the creation myth of the Mongolian Buryat (Buriat) people of the Lake Baikal region of Siberia, the Creator, Sombov, made people out of clay and covered them with warm wool, but decided not to give them life until he had found souls for them in heaven. He departed on his mission, leaving a dog to watch over the clay humans. At this time dogs had no fur and constantly shivered in the cold. Along came the devil, Shiktur, who promised the dog a fur coat if he would show him the new humans. After an argument, the dog gave in and revealed the clay figures. Immediately, Shiktur, desiring to leave his mark on creation, spit on the figures. When Sombov returned with souls, he was upset to find that his creation had been fouled. Wherever the trickster's spit had touched the humans, the wool in which the creator had covered them had to be removed. This left the humans—especially the females—with hair protecting only certain parts of their bodies. Sombov was furious at the dog for letting Shiktur corrupt his creation, so he gave the dog fur, but caused him, nevertheless, to shiver forever in the cold.

The central Asian myths, with their interfering trickster/devils, express the sense that whatever the Creator's original intentions, imperfection finds its way into life and contributes to what we are.

North America (Sioux, Maidu, Crow): Coyote

As in many cultures, the Native American trickster is associated with animals. In the Pacific Northwest he is typically Raven. In the Plains he is often Iktome the Spider. Throughout the continent his favorite incarnation is as Coyote. Many Coyote stories feature his overwhelming sexual appetite and the amoral means by which he satisfies it. More often the myths present the trickster as the butt of his own tricks or as an underminer of the Creator's work who introduces humans to the ambiguous reality of life.

The Sioux of the Great Plains tell this folk tale involving two tricksters, Coyote and Iktome. It seems that Coyote and the Spider were walking around one day when they noticed a large rock named Iya who was related to the spirit world. Wanting to keep on the good side of the rock and feeling generous that day, Coyote draped his cloak over Iya, saying, "Brother, this will keep you warm if the weather turns." When later the weather did, in fact, turn into a rain and sleet storm and Coyote and Iktome took shelter in a cave, Coyote had a change of mind. He asked Iktome to go back to the rock to retrieve the cloak. "Iya doesn't really need it," he said. Iktome went back to the rock and asked for the cloak, but Iya refused to part with it. "A gift given is a gift given," he said. "And besides, I like it." When Iktome reported all this, Coyote was furious. He rushed back to the rock and demanded his cloak back. But Iya answered as he had to Iktome: "A gift given is a gift given." Now even angrier, Coyote grabbed the cloak, shouting, "That takes care of that!" The rock answered, "Don't be so sure."

After the storm, the two tricksters were sunning themselves when they heard a strange noise. It was as if something was rolling along. Soon they saw what it was. Iya was rolling toward them. They ran, but the chase was relentless. When Iktome realized they were about to be caught, he saved himself by becoming his spider form and escaping down a hole. But Coyote was not so fortunate; the rock simply rolled over him, leaving him flattened out on the ground. A white man came along later and thought the flattened mass was a rug, so he took it home. When the white man woke up the next day, his wife told him she had seen his new Indian rug running away.

In a myth told by a Northern California tribe, the Maidu, Coyote introduced death itself into creation, much as the serpent had in the Garden of Eden. In the beginning, according to the myth, the Creator made a perfect world. But soon Coyote and his pet, Rattlesnake, came out of a hole in the ground and watched the Creator making animals and people out of clay. Coyote thought he could make people too, so he made some. But his people were imperfect, because he could not help laughing at them. Meanwhile, the Creator was continuing to make his perfect world—a world in which there would always be food and no one would have to work. He told the people that if a person became old, they only had to jump into the lake nearby to become young again.

When one day Coyote came to visit the people, they told him how good life was. But Coyote said, "This world isn't so great; I can show you something even better." Then he told the people that getting old and sick was, in fact, a good thing. And so was death. The people were confused by this. Coyote said a footrace would make everything clear. Meanwhile, Coyote's pet, Rattlesnake, hid in a hole just alongside the route of the proposed race, with his head just above ground. The race began with one runner leading the pack. This was Coyote's own son. Rattlesnake bit the boy as he passed by. The boy got sick and died. The people thought the boy was sleeping, but Coyote knew his son was dead—the first death in creation—and he shed the first tears in creation. Coyote told the people his son was dead, and as he dug a grave for him, he explained that death would be the end of each person's life, that jumping in the lake would no longer preserve life.

The Crow Indians have a creation myth that features the Creator, Old Man Coyote, and a figure called Little Coyote. Old Man Coyote realized he had only made male humans, so he made some females, and everyone got busy multiplying. Everything was fine until one day Old Man Coyote came across a miniature version of himself. "Who are you?" he asked. "I don't know, Big Brother; I'm just here," said Little Coyote. Then the little one began to make suggestions to his bigger self about the creation. "You've only made humans and ducks," he said. So Old Man Coyote set about making all kinds of animals and, acting like a true culture hero, he taught the people and animals how to dance, how to hunt, how to cook, how to make shelters, and how to live in a proper way together. But now Little Coyote got jealous of the people, and he did a bad thing. Like the Sumerian Enki, he gave the people many languages so they could not understand each other. This led to wars and many misunderstandings between tribes. So the world goes, thanks to Little Coyote, the trickster. This myth, like other trickster myths, speaks to the duality in both human nature and creation itself.

Mesoamerica (Aztec): Huehuecóyotl

The Codex Borbonicus, an Aztec codex composed by Aztec priests around the time of the Spanish conquest, describes a Mesoamerican version of a coyote trickster. Huehuecóyotl (or

Ueuecoyotl) is a dancing coyote who has human hands and feet. For the Aztecs, the coyote and, therefore, Huehuecóyotl, represented wisdom and male sexuality. Other sixteenth-century codexes depict Huehuecóyotl as a clownish figure who played tricks on both gods and humans. Most of his tricks were relatively harmless practical jokes, but he could also be destructive, like his North American cousin. He could cause wars between clans and tribes, and he could use his shapeshifting powers to achieve selfish ends. As in the case of other tricksters, his tricks could sometimes backfire, making a fool of him. In keeping with his trickster role, Huehuecóyotl had many lovers, including Temazcalteci, the goddess of sweat baths, and Xochiquetzal, the goddess of love and sexuality.

Greece: Hermes

A major Greek deity, known as the messenger of the gods, was Hermes (the Roman Mercury), the "mercurial" son of Zeus and the nymph Maia. A lesser-known aspect of this god was his role as somewhat of a trickster. Two elements of the trickster profile apply particularly to Hermes—his association with theft and his association with sexuality.

The myths of Hermes tell us that the god was born in the cave where he was conceived. He emerged from his mother as a fully developed child and left the cave. Almost immediately, he came across a tortoise, and he decided to put it to good use. He killed the animal and used its shell as the main body of an instrument now known as the lyre. The clever child then sang beautiful songs to the accompaniment of the lyre—songs that enchanted his listeners.

Now Hermes decided that he needed meat. His appetite overcame any qualms he might have had, and he devised a plan to steal his older brother Apollo's cattle. Hiding his footprints with special sandals he had made, the boy tricked the cows into following him to a hidden place, where he butchered two of them. He then invented a process whereby rubbing sticks together made fire, and he cooked some of the meat. Now, still a baby, after all, he returned to his cradle in his mother's cave. His mother knew he had been up to something and scolded him. Meanwhile, Apollo was furious when he learned of the theft of his cattle. With help from a witness who had seen a child leading cattle away, Apollo found his way to Maia's cave and confronted the baby Hermes. Hermes denied any guilt, pleading childhood innocence, but Apollo recognized the child as a born thief and took him to Mount Olympus for Zeus's judgment. Zeus listened to Apollo's case and then laughed at Hermes's obvious lies before ordering the child to lead Apollo to the place where he had hidden the cattle. When Apollo retrieved his cattle, Hermes took up the lyre he had invented and played so beautifully that Apollo forgave him for everything and announced that the boy would become the messenger of the gods. Hermes gave the lyre to Apollo, who became its most talented player. Hermes vowed never again to be a thief.

The sexual aspect of Hermes the trickster has to do with what came to be known as his ability as messenger to penetrate boundaries—between life and death, between this world and the next. This ultimate seductive power was symbolized by the ubiquitous *herms*—stone columns often with the god's head and erect phallus—that stood as protective talismans before Greek homes and other buildings. Hermes's sexuality is also demonstrated in the myth of his relationship with his stepsister Aphrodite, with whom he parented the androgynous child Hermaphroditus.

The Hermes trickster myth speaks directly to the modern psychological interpretation of the trickster as a reflection of the preconsciousness state of the child. The child has no superego, as it were, no reason to deny itself pleasure, even if that pleasure comes at the expense of others. In the Hermes myth the child moves into adult consciousness through the actions of Apollo and Zeus and emerges as a positive force among the Olympians.

Norselands (Iceland): Loki

A much less sympathetic trickster than Hermes is the Norse god Loki. The *Prose Edda* reveals him as a clever and cruel shapeshifting being who is capable of extreme cruelty and whose actions threaten the very existence of the Aesir-dominated world. Loki's appetites—especially his sexual drives—are typical of tricksters. No sense of morality tempers his actions. Married to Sigyn, he nevertheless has many affairs. By the monstrous Angrbooa, he is the father of Hel, the goddess of death, the destructive wolf Fenrir, and the world serpent Jörmungandr, who surrounds the world and kills the great god Thor (who kills him in turn) at Ragnarok.

An example of Loki's shapeshifting is his becoming a mare so he can mate with a stallion and become the mother of Odin's eight-legged horse, Sleipnir. In this act he uses his cunning and his creativity to help Odin and the other gods, the Aesir. More often, however, he is destructive, and in the end, he has to be physically restrained by them.

One of Loki's most destructive acts is his involvement with the death of the much-loved god Baldr the Beautiful, the gentle son of Odin. Baldr dreamt that he would be killed. To prevent that, Baldr's mother, Frigg, convinced everything and everyone on earth to promise not to harm her son. Somehow, however, Frigg managed to miss the tiny mistletoe. Now, thinking Baldr was safe, the gods began throwing things at him for fun. Loki entered the game, but not for fun. He disguised himself as a female and chatted with Frigg, who told him about the missed mistletoe. Right away Loki went out to the woods and plucked some of the plant, which he gave to Baldr's brother, Hodr. He suggested that Hodr throw the plant at his brother as part of the fun the gods were having. But Hodr was blind, so Loki guided his hand, and the mistletoe hit Baldr in the heart, causing the god's instant death. The gods were all saddened at Baldr's death, and Odin took it as a sign of the coming end of the world. Frigg begged for a volunteer to travel to the land of the death goddess to rescue her beloved son. Another son, Hermod, agreed to go, and when he found Baldr, Hel told him his brother could be released, but only if everything and everyone in the world would weep for the dead god. Odin ordered this universal mourning and everyone and everything complied—except for a giantess, who was, in fact, a disguise for the shapeshifting trickster. "Let Hel keep what is hers," the giantess cried. So poor Baldr had to stay in the land of Hel. Odin's fear that Baldr's death foreshadowed Ragnarok, the end of the world, turned out to be true. Loki's malevolent trick destroyed creation itself.

China: the Monkey King

Whatever his original source in Chinese mythology, the trickster Sun Wukong, the Monkey King, is known to us primarily as depicted in *Journey to the West*, a sixteenth-century Chinese novel by the scholar Cheng'en. The novel is based loosely on the journey during the Tang dynasty of the Buddhist monk Xuanzang from China to India to obtain authentic Buddhist sutras.

The Monkey King had several familiar trickster powers. He was a shapeshifter who, at will, could become any number of different animals. He could control the elements of nature and, most of all, he recognized no power greater than himself and possessed gargantuan self-esteem.

Sun Wukong was born of a stone egg as a monkey. After helping his fellow monkeys, he was made their king. Early on, he began work on avoiding the whole cycle of life and death. Eventually he succeeded. Once immortal, he followed the trickster pattern by stealing. From the Dragon King he stole the golden-hooped rod that became his primary weapon. Like other tricksters, the Monkey King could travel between the worlds of life and death, and he assumed power even over the rulers of the underworld. Wary of the trickster's power, the Jade Emperor, king of heaven, appointed him to a heavenly position. The position was too minor to satisfy the Monkey King, and he made so much trouble that the emperor named him "Great Sage, Equal to Heaven." Even this did not satisfy Wukong, and he committed trickster deeds such as stealing the Queen Mother's food at one of her banquets, which he attended uninvited. He was imprisoned for his misdeeds but easily escaped. Finally, the Buddha decide to take control of the situation. He bet Wukong that he could not escape from the palm of his hand. Although he could leap instantly for thousands of miles and was sure he could easily leap off the Buddha's hand, when Wukong did so he found that he was still on the sacred palm, and he was sentenced to 500 years under a mountain. Again, as in the case of many other tricksters, the Monkey King ultimately paid dearly for his unbridled powers.

Polynesia: Maui

In various parts of Polynesia stories are told of Maui, a sometimes comic, sometimes serious character who is both a trickster and a hero. Maui was an accomplished thief. In Maori mythology, for instance, he stole fire from the underworld, joining many tricksters who use their cunning to steal fire. In a Samoan myth, the underworld theft of fire involved Maui (Ti'iti'i) defeating the earthquake god in physical combat after first tricking him into giving him a tiny bit of fire. And like other fire-stealing tricksters in the world, he acts as a culture hero, giving the fire to people for their use. In many Polynesian islands, Maui is also said to have captured the sun to make the days longer for the people.

Also in keeping with the trickster tradition, Maui was a notoriously sexual being. In one story, the beautiful goddess Hina was living with the long and slimy eel, Te Tuna. Disappointed in the eel as a lover, Hina went in search of a better and more productive love life. Arriving in the land of the Male Principle Clan, she announced her desire for a lover. The men were afraid of Te Tuna, however, and sent her away. Desperate now, Hina traveled to the land of the Maui Clan, and Maui took Hina as his wife. Maui and Hina lived together passionately for a long time, but one day some of the people told Te Tuna what was going on, suggesting that he should take back his wife. Then the people warned Maui that Te Tuna was on his way, intent on revenge. Te Tuna approached from the sea, exposing a penis so large that it caused a tidal wave. Maui revealed his own member and with it calmed the wave. For a while Te Tuna and Maui shared Hina, but finally they fought in a highly sexualized battle in which the two entered each other. Finally, Maui cut off Te Tuna's head and buried it. From that spot the coconut tree emerged, providing food for the people.

Some Maori people tell how Maui longed for immortality for himself and for the people and tried a desperate trick to achieve his goal. Being, like all tricksters, a shapeshifter, he turned himself into a worm and entered the underworld goddess, Hine-nui-te-oo, by way of her vagina. He planned to travel all the way through the goddess and exit through her mouth, thus overcoming death itself. Unfortunately, the trick failed, however, and even though the goddess was asleep, her obsidian vaginal teeth crushed Maui, ending both his life and the hope of immortality.

As in so many other trickster myths, Maui's plans end up in spectacular failure. The attempt itself, however, reveals the role of the trickster as the representative of the human desire to break through the restrictions of conventionality and nature itself.

Australia: (Wurundjeri) Crow

Another trickster who, like Prometheus and Maui, steals fire for the good of the people is the Australian Aborigine Crow. In a story told by the Wurundjeri people of the Kulin Nation in Victoria, near what is Melbourne a Dreamtime trickster whose animal form is Crow steals fire from a strange group of seven known as the Karatgurk Women. These women carried fire on their digging sticks and used it to cook their yams. In those days, the people did not have fire and did not cook their yams. But Crow came along, ate a piece of cooked yam left behind by the women, and decided it was much better than the raw yams he was used to. He asked the women to share their fire so that he could tell the people how to cook things. But the women refused, so Crow decided to resort to his natural trickster's cunning to get what he wanted. He gathered some snakes and put them in an anthill.

7. A nineteenth-century mask, or *kara*, made of turtle shell, wood, feathers, and other natural materials represents an Australian Aborigine culture hero and trickster, who turns ordinary objects into elements of ritual power.

Then he called the women and told them he had discovered that ant larvae tasted even better than yams. The greedy women started digging immediately for the larvae, and, of course, the snakes attacked them. The women fought back, hitting the snakes with their sticks with such force that they produced sparks and hot coals, which Crow then hid away in a bag. When the women discovered the theft, they chased the trickster, who simply took his bird form and flew to the top of a tree and crowed at them. Soon people and other animals gathered around Crow's tree and demanded that he share the fire so they could cook. Crow threw some of the live coals down to the people. The result was a great fire, which threatened the land until another bird, Eaglehawk, and his shaman bird helpers managed to put it out. Now the people could use fire for proper cooking. As for the Karatgurk Women, they became the Pleiades, lighting the sky with their glowing digging sticks.

Africa: Ananse/Legba

African tricksters, like those of other animist cultures, are highly creative beings who sometimes challenge the creator god to aid humans, acting as culture heroes, putting human needs above divine arbitrariness. But, more often, like tricksters elsewhere, African tricksters have large and uncontrollable appetites for sex, food, and power and generally can serve as metaphors for human self-centeredness. They are known particularly for their trickery as thieves.

An example of the trickster's contradictory role is Hlakanyana, a Bantu figure who had once participated with the high god in the creation process but later undermined that process with cunning and thievery in the interest of his people, as well as in his self-interest. Another Bantu trickster is Dikithi, famous for having one arm, one leg, and one eye, who sometimes stole things for the people, but was better known for stealing other people's cattle for himself.

Among the best-known African tricksters are Legba (Eshu) and Ananse. In the New World they took such forms as Papa Legba in Haitian Voodoo and "Aunt Nancy" or Brer Rabbit in the American South. Legba or Eshu, a spirit figure in Yoruba and Fon mythology, is associated with fertility. Like the Greek Hermes, he can penetrate the spirit world, and in some places, such as Dahomey (Benin), his phallic symbol, like the one on Hermes's *herm*, is placed in front of houses to ensure fertility and protection from evil spirits. Legba was present at the very beginning of creation. Some say he was the Creator's son and that, at first, he acted as a culture hero, teaching the people in the frequent absences of the Creator. When bad things happened, Legba was blamed, and when good things happened, the Creator was praised. This irritated Legba and he confronted his father, complaining about his treatment. "That's just the way things are and always will be," said the Creator. Now even more angry, Legba decided to use his cunning to achieve revenge. He lied to his father, telling him he had heard that thieves were planning to steal yams from the god's famous garden. The Creator was furious, saying that any such thief would be executed. One night, Legba stole into his sleeping father's house, took his father's sandals, put them on, walked into the sacred garden, took all the yams from it, and then replaced the sandals by the Creator's bed. The next morning, he went to the house and told his father that the yams had been stolen, but that the thief had left sandal prints. So, the great god called everyone together to see whose sandals would match the prints in the garden. But the prints were much larger than the sandals of any human. Then Legba made a daring suggestion. He said to his father, "Maybe you walked in the garden in your sleep and took the yams." "Impossible," cried the god, and he placed his sandaled feet on the sandal prints in the garden. The fit was perfect, and the people began grumbling about the Creator stealing from himself. Now the Creator realized that his cunning son had tricked him. Furious, he departed the world for good, leaving Legba in charge.

Ananse, the Spider, is a popular trickster in many parts of western Africa. As the spider, he weaves stories and many of the stories are about himself. Ananse was the son of the sky god creator Nyame or Wulbari or some other god. His mother was said to be the earth goddess. Like Legba, Ananse was at first a culture hero, teaching the people how to live properly in his father's creation. But Ananse, like all tricksters, had an agenda of his own and was not above tricking even the high god to achieve his goals. According to some Ashanti people, it was Ananse who created both the sun and the first people, but he also stole the god's daughter.

In a Krachi tale, the Creator, Wulbari, heard Ananse bragging that he was much smarter than the Creator himself. The god decided to teach his son a lesson. He sent him off to earth to find something. But he never said what the something was. "If you're so smart, you should be able to figure out what it is you should look for," he said. Now the Spider used his cunning and the trickster's ability to change shape. He went to earth, took feathers from all kinds of birds, and attached them to himself. Then he flew back to heaven disguised as a bird. Wulbari saw this beautiful bird and was amazed by it. He asked the animals what kind of bird it was, and they said they had no idea but that Ananse might know. "But I can't ask him," said the god, "because I've sent him to earth to look for something." "Oh," said the animals. "What did you tell him to look for?" "I didn't tell him," answered Wulbari, "but I had in mind the sun, the moon, and darkness." Of course, Ananse, disguised as the beautiful bird, heard this conversation. He immediately left, collected the sun, the moon, and darkness, placed them in a sack, and returned to Wulbari. When he took the darkness out of the sack nobody could see anything. When he took the moon out they could see something but not much, and when he brought out the sun they could see everything. So it was that Wulbari the Creator was outsmarted by the clever Ananse.

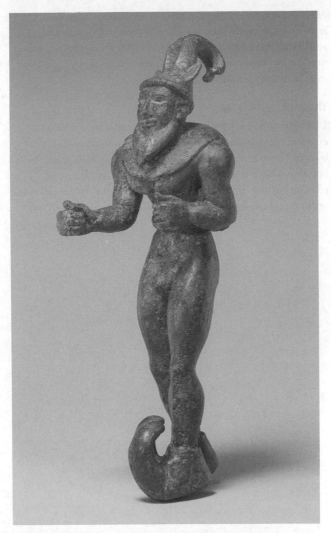

8. Sporting ibex horns, a raptor-skin scarf, and upturned shoes, this metalwork sculpture from about 3000 BCE represents a trickster of the Elamite culture in what is now Iran.

African trickster myths, like African mythology in general, tend to express a somewhat skeptical view of powerful deities and the world they have created. The world in African mythology is a precarious place where a trickster's cunning is appreciated and even necessary for survival.

The trickster and us

Ultimately, the trickster is a kind of escape valve. He relieves creation of a sentimental and unrealistic view of itself. The trickster represents the reality of the contradictions in our lives, between what we call good and evil, life and death, social convention and individual appetites. The trickster embodies the tension that permeates art, relationships, the seasons—life itself.

Chapter 5
The hero

The dictionary definition of a hero is a person who is celebrated for courage and achievements, particularly in relation to cultures or nations. George Washington is a hero of the American Revolution. Joan of Arc is a French national hero. The definition of a mythic hero is more complicated. There are many types of mythic hero. Often associated with creation myths are culture heroes, sent or left behind by creators to teach humans how to live properly. White Buffalo Calf Woman is such a figure for the Sioux Indians. The Great Spirit sends her to teach the people sacred rituals and proper behavior. Many tricksters turn out to be culture heroes who use their magical powers to steal elements such as fire from the creators for the benefit of humans. There are well-known epic heroes such as Odysseus or Aeneas, equally famous tragic heroes such as Oedipus, and flood heroes such as Utnapishtim and Noah. Saint George and Siegfried kill dragons and other monsters for the benefit of their people. Religious heroes possess revolutionary spiritual understandings that make them saviors of their people. The Buddha, Moses, Muhammad, and Jesus are such heroes. And there are the questing heroes. The knights of King Arthur's Round Table who search for the Holy Grail are examples. Some heroes are historical or legendary figures to whom mythic characteristics are applied later by their followers. Miraculous conceptions and ascensions to heaven can do much to elevate historical figures into mythic ones.

9. A nineteenth-century work by the Arapaho painter Frank Henderson, in which warriors on horseback are leaving for war, is an example of ledger art, in which Native Americans narrated important events by depicting them on paper.

Most of our mythic heroes have been revealed to us in literary works. Unlike the deity, creation, and trickster myths, hero myths are typically attributed to individual authors. Whatever the source of the Greek heroes, for instance, as we have come to know them, they are the inventions of Homer and the Greek tragedians. Many of the heroes of India are brought to life in an epic said to be the work of a poet named Vyasa. What we know of the Roman hero Aeneas is in Virgil's epic named after him.

Inevitably, the study of the mythic hero must take into consideration the works of several scholars who relate the hero's life to human psychology. The best known of these scholars are Otto Rank, Lord FitzRoy Raglan, and Joseph Campbell, each of whom adds significant elements to a comparative understanding of the elements that make up the universal or archetypal elements of what Campbell called the "hero with a thousand faces," or, to use the word coined by James Joyce, the heroic *monomyth*. Campbell's monomyth includes a miraculous conception and birth, a significant childhood initiation, a quest, a descent to the underworld, and a return or rebirth/resurrection, familiar elements in the biographies of the world's mythic heroes.

Mesopotamia (Sumer, Akkad, Babylon): Gilgamesh

Perhaps the earliest of the literary mythic heroes, Gilgamesh is generally considered to have been an actual king of the Sumerian city of Uruk sometime in the third millennium BCE. His mythical history begins with several fragmentary Sumerian tales, followed in the early second millennium by a more complete version of what has come to be known as the *Epic of Gilgamesh*, written in the Semitic Akkadian language. A later, more complete Babylonian version is commonly attributed to a scribe named Sin-leqi-unnini, and a still-later seventh-century BCE Babylonian version was discovered in the Assyrian Library of Assurbanipal in Nineveh.

Like many mythic heroes, Gilgamesh had direct ties to the divine. His father was said to have been the human priest-king Lugalbanda, but his mother was the mother goddess Ninsumun (Ninsun), the Lady of the Cows. Although the son of a goddess, Gilgamesh's human status was clearly expressed in his imperfections and his inability to overcome death, the ultimate definer of humanity as opposed to divinity.

As a young king, Gilgamesh displays the fault of arrogance, causing the gods to send the bestial Enkidu to challenge him. In a wrestling match, Gilgamesh barely defeats Enkidu, and the two men become inseparable friends. Together the pair take on the role of heroic monster slayer by fighting and killing the terrible giant Humbaba, guardian of the Cedar Forest of the gods. In the course of the battle, Enkidu is wounded, and eventually he dies, perhaps providing the incentive for what becomes Gilgamesh's central heroic adventure, the quest for immortality. In the course of the quest, Gilgamesh must pass through what is, in effect, an archetypal underworld in which, for instance, he must convince the terrifying scorpion people to allow him to pass through a long, dark tunnel. In the quest, Gilgamesh is detained but assisted by the beautiful Siduri, who has mythical "sisters" in figures such as

Calypso and Circe in Homer's much later epic, the *Odyssey*. Finally arriving at the River of Death, the Sumerian equivalent of the River Styx, Gilgamesh is ferried across by the ferryman Urshanabi, whose Greek counterpart will be Charon. Once across the river, Gilgamesh meets the Mesopotamian flood hero Utnapishtim (Sumerian Ziasudra), who will teach the questing hero that the gods alone are the guardians of immortality.

After describing the great flood and his role in it, Utnapishtim (the Mesopotamian Noah) challenges Gilgamesh to stay awake for six days and seven nights, but the hero, exhausted by his journey, immediately falls asleep. During each day of his sleep Utnapishtim's wife bakes a loaf of bread and leaves it by the sleeper. When the hero awakens, he sees the now moldy bread and understands the purpose of Utnapishtim's challenge. He is human, and immortality is beyond human powers. As a consolation, Utnapishtim gives Gilgamesh a plant that will at least provide eternal youth. But even this prize eludes the all-too-human hero, who again falls asleep, allowing a serpent to steal the plant. Gilgamesh returns home to Uruk where, presumably having accepted his mortality and its limitations, he encourages the ferryman Urshanabi to admire the beauty of the city walls he has constructed. Gilgamesh's heroic attempt to overcome the limitations of human life serves as a model for many of the heroes who are his mythological descendants in other cultures.

Israel: Moses

The five books of the Pentateuch (Torah) of the Bible are traditionally attributed to Judaism's greatest hero, Moses. And Moses's heroic saga is a primary subject, especially of the book of Exodus. Heroes often arise when cultures are experiencing threats to their very existence. This is the case with Moses. The story begins with a birth that, while not miraculous, is highly unusual. The people known as the Hebrews, who were enslaved in Egypt, had become so numerous that the pharaoh decided to reduce the population by ordering that all newborn Hebrew boys be thrown into the Nile to drown. Meanwhile, a Hebrew man, Amram, married a Hebrew woman, Jochebed, and they had a child. Hoping to save her baby from Pharoah's massacre, Jochebed put the child into a watertight basket and set the basket afloat in the Nile. The baby's sister, Miriam, watched as a daughter of the pharaoh found the basket and immediately adopted the newborn baby it contained. Miriam then introduced Jochebed to the pharaoh, who accepted her as the child's wet nurse without realizing that she was the boy's mother.

In his adulthood Moses began to reveal his heroic role when he killed an Egyptian who had been mistreating two Hebrew slaves. Forced to flee Egypt, he came to Midian in the northwestern Arabian Peninsula and eventually married Zipporah, the daughter of a Midian priest. Moses lived in Midian for forty years while his people continued to suffer in Egypt. But one day Moses climbed a mountain, and there, in a clear sign of what would be his close link to divinity, a bush caught fire and a voice that came from it introduced himself to Moses as the "I Am, the god of your fathers," Abraham, Isaac, and Jacob.

In many hero sagas the hero embarks on his major quest after receiving a significant call to action from a higher power. In this case Yahweh instructs Moses to return to Egypt and lead his people, the Hebrews, to the land of Canaan. Like many heroes, Moses at first refuses the call, claiming his insignificance and his powerlessness to bring the Hebrews out of Egypt. But when Yahweh promises to be with him, Moses agrees and returns to Egypt to take up his calling. So begins Moses's heroic quest for a "promised land" for his people. On his quest he is given powerful signs of support from his god. When the Egyptian army pursues the escaping Hebrews, Yahweh parts the Red Sea (or Sea of Reeds) to allow the Hebrews to pass through it and then releases the waters to drown the pursuing Egyptians. When later the Hebrews are starving in the wilderness, he sends *manna*—sacred bread—on which Moses's people feed for forty years. And Yahweh chooses Moses as the recipient of his gift of the Ten Commandments and the Torah, delivered on Mount Sinai. Although Moses succeeds in leading his people, he himself never reaches the Promised Land. But Yahweh shows it to him from Mount Nebu in Moab before the great hero dies at age 120.

Moses is not so much a mythical or archetypal hero as he is a legendary or, some would say, historical one. While unusual, his conception and birth are not miraculous, neither of his biological parents is divine, and he does not descend to the underworld or rise from the dead. His heroism is based in his being chosen by the deity as the leader of the Hebrews in their quest for the Promised Land, a quest ultimately central to the foundation of Judaism.

India: Gautama Buddha

Another hero associated with a major religion is Siddhartha Gautama Buddha (or Sakyamuni Buddha, because he was born to a clan known as the Sakyas). The many schools of Buddhism have produced various versions of the Buddha's life. Some have concentrated on the historical figure born in about 563 BCE in Lubimi near the India–Nepal border. Others have included supernatural events that suggest mythology rather than history.

One legendary version of Gautama Buddha's life describes a miraculous conception. According to that version, during the full moon at the midsummer festival, Queen Maha Maya had this dream. She was carried by four guardian angels to the Himalaya Mountains, who placed her under a great sal tree. Then the wives of the angels came and took her to Anotatta Lake, where they bathed her, washing away all her human stain, making her, in effect, immaculate. Then they placed her on a couch in a golden temple. Meanwhile, the future Buddha became a beautiful white elephant and entered the temple. He walked three times around his mother's couch, tapping her on her right side. When she awoke, Queen Maha Maya told her husband, King Suddhodana, of her dream and he asked wise men to interpret it. The men said a child had planted himself in the womb of the queen and that the child would become a great buddha. In this way, Gautama Buddha was conceived.

The queen carried the future Buddha (*bodhisattva*) in her womb for ten months with no discomfort. When it was time for his birth, she decided to go to the home of her family in Devedaha. On the way there she came to a grove of sal trees, the Lumbini grove, and there, standing up, holding on to a branch of a sal tree, she gave birth to Gautama. Since her womb was a sacred temple, having been occupied by the future Buddha, it could never be used again. So Queen Maha Maya died.

The most important event in the life of the future Buddha was his achievement of enlightenment under a sacred fig tree known as the Bodhi (enlightenment) Tree at Bodh Gaya in Bihar, India. During this event several mythological elements reveal the Buddha as an archetypal hero. Sitting under the tree, Gautama decided to meditate until he had achieved full knowledge of life and its meaning, thus becoming no longer a bodhisattva but a Buddha, a fully awakened being. During his time under the tree the future Buddha was tempted by Mara the Fiend. Mara first took the form of a messenger who presented a letter from his Sakya relatives warning the bodhisattva that enemies had stolen his possessions and his wife and that he needed to return home to restore order. The bodhisattva refused, noting that it was lust, malice, and cowardice that had caused the loss of his wife and possessions, making it all the more important that he seek enlightenment. Mara now used all of his forces against the bodhisattva—even a violent storm and flood—but these had no effect. Mara resorted to a shower of rocks, poisoned weapons, and fire, but these all landed at the bodhisattva's feet as beautiful flowers or became a fine canopy over his head. Finally, Mara commanded his enemy to leave his seat under the Bodhi Tree.

But the bodhisattva refused, pointing out that Mara had accomplished no virtuous act, acquired no supreme knowledge, and done nothing to achieve the world's salvation. After failing to outdo Gautama with other arguments, Mara tried to tempt him by having beautiful women dance lasciviously before him. These women could be his, said Mara, and he could be lord of the earth itself if only he would give up his quest for enlightenment. But the bodhisattva was unmoved by temptations of the flesh. "Pleasure is as brief as a lightning flash," he said. Mara's promise was birth, sickness, age, and death. The bodhisattva's promise was enlightenment. Mara was thus defeated, and the bodhisattva continued on his truer path to enlightenment. In his final hours under the Bodhi Tree he achieved that goal and became the Buddha. After his enlightenment he became a traveling teacher, who taught people the truth he had learned.

Israel: Jesus

However he is viewed theologically, philosophically, or historically, the man we know of as Jesus, probably born near the beginning of the Common Era in Roman-occupied Israel, is depicted as an archetypal hero in the biblical narratives of his life and in the traditions that have developed around him, in some cases, long after his death. The New Testament books—Gospels—by men identified as Mark, Matthew, Luke, and John, present Jesus as the Messiah, or Christ, the long-promised savior of the Jewish people, and each of the books contains events that resemble those associated with other heroes in world mythology. These events are central to the development of what became the religion of Christianity.

The first of the mythological events is the conception and birth. Matthew and Luke emphasize Jesus's direct association with divinity. By claiming that he was conceived by a virgin, Mary, without sexual intercourse, through the agency of the Holy Spirit, these gospelers provided the church fathers with the Christian doctrine that defines Jesus as the "son of God."

The Christmas story, the story of Jesus's birth, in which Mary gives birth in the simple stable and lays her child in a manger, is made even more significant in the nonbiblical church doctrine of the Immaculate Conception, according to which Mary herself was said to have been conceived by her parents without sin. Mary's heroism is made still clearer in another nonbiblical doctrine—the Assumption—according to which, at the end of her earthly life, she was raised into Heaven to reign there as queen (*Regina Caeli*).

Jesus's first trial as a hero is contained in the story told only by Matthew, that wise men—perhaps astrologers—from the east came to worship the young Jesus as "King of the Jews." Apparently, they had determined the existence of the child by examining the stars and finding one that they followed to Israel. There they visited King Herod and asked for advice on where to find the new "king." Fearing a potential rival, Herod, when his advisors told him of a prophecy regarding the birth of the Messiah in Bethlehem, decreed that all male babies in Bethlehem should be killed. Fortunately, a dream led Mary's husband, Joseph, to take the child out of Israel into Egypt to avoid his certain death. This story of the massacre of the innocents is reminiscent of Pharaoh's similar decree regarding the male children of the enslaved Hebrews. In many hero myths, the child hero is threatened by evil kings who represent the forces of the status quo that stand against the new priorities represented by the hero.

Jesus's adult life is marked by many miraculous events—the changing of water into wine at a wedding feast in Cana, the healing of the sick and the blind. And like the Buddha, who was tempted by Mara the Fiend, Jesus was tempted by Satan. Matthew, Mark, and Luke all tell how Satan offered Jesus earthly power in return for allegiance to him. In each case Jesus resisted his tempter.

The central miraculous event in Jesus's life and in the formation of Christianity is his resurrection. All four gospels tell how Jesus, after being crucified, rose from the dead. All but Mark tell of his physical appearance to his followers after his resurrection. The events leading to the crucifixion and death are those of the Christian Holy Week, in which Jesus with his followers enters Jerusalem, establishes the sacred rite of bread and wine in the "Last Supper" in the "upper room," is tried for blasphemy, and is crucified. The resurrection is celebrated at Easter, the feast that, for Christians, marks the success of the ancient quest expressed, for instance, in the myths of Gilgamesh and Osiris, for immortality or eternal life. So it is that, according to the four gospelers and the book of Acts, Jesus ascended bodily to Heaven to reign there with God.

As a mythological hero, Jesus fulfills the requirements of the "hero with a thousand faces." He is conceived and born miraculously, one of his parents is divine, his life is a quest, and he experiences and overcomes death, returns to life, and ascends to Heaven.

Iran (Persia): Zoroaster

Still another hero whose life and teaching formed the basis of a new religion was Zoroaster (Zarathustra), a prophet and reformer who lived in Persia (present-day Iran) sometime between 1000 and 500 BCE. The canonical theology, teachings, and tenets associated with what became the religion of Zoroastrianism are contained in the Avesta (Zend-Avesta). Other less sacred texts, such as the tenth-century Denkard and apocryphal folk traditions, present Zoroaster in a traditionally heroic context.

In the noncanonical version of his life story, Zoroaster's conception and birth are unusual if not technically miraculous. It is said that his father, Pouroshaspa, mixed milk with the sacred *Haoma* (*sauma*, Sanskrit *soma*) plant and shared the drink with his wife, Dughdova (Dughda), before they came together to conceive the prophet. In the sixth month of her pregnancy Dughdova dreams that good and bad spirits are fighting over the embryo of Zoroaster. When a wicked spirit rips the child from her womb, a good spirit defeats his evil counterpart and replaces the embryo in the womb. This struggle foreshadows Zoroaster's teachings regarding the essential duality of the universe—the struggle between the good god, Ahura Mazda, and the negative god, Angra Mainyu. A wise dream interpreter tells Dughdova that her son is destined to be a great man who will have to face many trials. When the boy is born, he immediately looks about and laughs, a fact that suggests his uniqueness. Some magi tell the king, Duransarun, that the child born to the house of Pouroshaspa will be a threat to his reign. The king immediately goes to the house and raises a dagger to stab the baby. But miraculously, his raised hand becomes paralyzed in midair, and he leaves. Soon evil forces steal the child and take him to a desert, intending to kill him. But Dughdova finds the child before he can be killed. Like King Herod in the Jesus myth, King Duransarun does not give up, however; he sends a herd of oxen to trample the baby to death, but the largest of the oxen takes the child to safety between its feet. When the king sends horses to do what the oxen have failed to do, the largest horse preserves the child just as the ox had done. Whatever Duransarun tries to do to him, the divine fire of Ahura Mazda within Zoroaster prevails.

Zoroaster left his parents' home at a young age after he had already become a priest. At the age of thirty he had an enlightenment experience during a spring festival. A sacred reality took the form of Vohu Manah (Proper Purpose) and taught the young prophet all about Ahura Mazda, Angra Mainyu, and the duality of nature and life. After this revelation and several other visions, Zoroaster devoted his life to teaching his people what he had learned and leading them to *Asha*, a concept of truth, righteousness, and order. Like the Buddha, Moses, and Jesus, with whom he shares many miracles and qualities, Zoroaster is a savior hero for his people.

China: Guanyin

Although generally depicted in China as the goddess of compassion, who is in India and Tibetan Buddhism the Bodhisattva Avalokitesvara, Guanyin plays a human role in Chinese legend and mythology that establishes her as a savior hero such as Moses, Jesus, the Buddha, and Zoroaster. As in the cases of the Buddha and Zoroaster, a dream plays a role in the legend of her conception.

It is said that Queen Yin, who was married to King Zhuang of Chu, dreamt one night that a beautiful crystal ball rolled into her stomach. Wise men interpreted the dream, saying a child of world-changing importance would be born to her. In fact, a child was born, and the royal couple named her Miai-San. As the child grew, she acted in ways that confused her parents. For one thing, she began to chant Buddhist sutras before she could really talk normally. Miai-San grew up, and because she was a girl, her father eventually decided it was necessary that she marry. But the girl refused marriage. She announced she would become a nun unless her marriage would solve the problem of sickness, aging, and death. In this decision Miai-San aligned herself with Gautama Buddha, who gave up the privileged life as a prince of the Sakyas to commit to the pursuit of enlightenment and the salvation of his people.

When he realized it would be impossible to meet his daughter's marriage requirements, the king let her go to a Buddhist nunnery but instructed the leaders there to give the girl the hardest work possible, hoping the pain caused by such work would make her change her mind. When forest animals around the nunnery began to help the girl with her chores, the king became so angry that he set fire to the building. But when Miai-San managed to extinguish the fire with her bare hands, the king accused her of witchery and condemned her to death. As in the cases of Jesus and Zoroaster, whose lives were threatened by evil kings, King Zhuang's plans

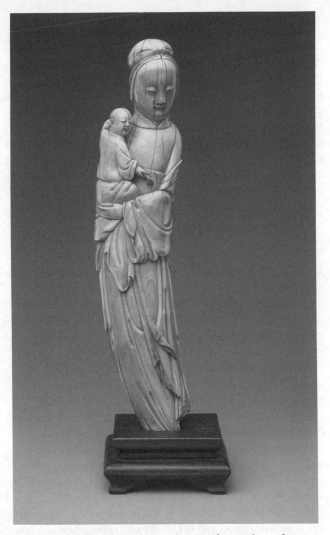

10. A sixteenth-century Ming dynasty ivory sculpture shows the great Bodhisattva Guanyin holding a child, emphasizing her role as a deity of mercy and compassion.

were foiled by the divine power that emanated from his daughter. When the executioner raised his axe to carry out the death sentence, the axe shattered before the blow could be administered. The same thing happened when the executioner tried to use his sword. Only then did Miai-San allow herself to be killed. Following other mythic heroes, Miai-San descended to hell. From there she wept in sorrow for the dead, and she used her mysterious powers to release many. Finally realizing his mistake and fearing for the continuance of his kingdom, King Zhuang allowed his daughter to return to life, and she did so, now becoming the Bodhisattva of mercy, Guanyin. The miraculous conception and deeds, the descent to hell, the quest for and achievement of enlightenment, and her overcoming of death all mark Guanyin as a mythic world hero.

India: Draupadi

The heroic Draupadi was the wife of all five leaders of the Pandava family in the great Sanskrit Indian epic, the Mahabharata. Traditionally, the epic is attributed to the sage Vyasa. Begun perhaps in about 400 BCE, it concerns events that were purported to have occurred several centuries earlier.

The twenty-sixth book of the epic describes Draupadi's miraculous birth. King Drupada of Panchala performed a sacrificial rite—a *yajna*—in the form of a fire. Two beings emerged from the fire. These were Dhrishtadyumna and his sister, Draupadi. As Draupadi emerged, fully grown and exceptionally beautiful, a divine voice announced that she would be the source of extraordinary events. When it came time for her to marry, she was betrothed to the Pandava hero Arjuna—the man whose discussion with Krishna is the subject of the great philosophical work, the Bhagavad Gita. Returning home with Draupadi and his brothers, Arjuna, playing a joke on his mother, Kunti, said he was returning home with many alms. By alms—*bheeksha*—he was actually referring to his bride. Without realizing this, Kunti ordered that Arjuna must share the alms with his brothers. Because the Pandavas never disobeyed their mother, Draupadi had to marry all five brothers.

Later, an extraordinary event made clear Draupadi's special connection to divine power and established her role as a true hero. One of the Pandava brothers, Yudhishthira, had foolishly used Draupadi as his ultimate stake in a gambling game of dice with an enemy, Dushasana. When Yudhishthira loses, Dushasana, hoping to humiliate both the Pandavas and their wife, demands that Draupadi, whom he has won in the game, be disrobed. But the god Krishna comes to her assistance. As her enemies unwind her sari, it becomes endless. Finally, when a huge pile of cloth lay on the floor and Draupadi was still clothed, the enemies of the Pandavas gave up. Then the pile of clothes miraculously burst into flames and disappeared, and the sky went dark and all the animals of the fields shrieked.

Draupadi spent years in exile with her husbands, and after the great war described at the end of the Mahabharata, she went with them to the Himalayas and walked to heaven, following the route of the many heroes who ascend to their divine sources.

Greece: Theseus

More than any mythological tradition, Greek mythology celebrates figures who can be defined clearly as archetypal heroes because of several familiar motifs. These motifs include the miraculous conception and/or birth, the direct connection to the divine, the quest for goals beyond the reach of ordinary humans, and the descent to and return from the underworld. One of the greatest of the Greek heroes is Theseus, essentially the national hero of Attica. His story is known to us primarily through Plutarch's *Life of Theseus*, a first-century CE work based on many earlier sources dating to the fifth and fourth centuries BCE and earlier.

Theseus was said to be the son of Aegeus, the king of Athens and Aethra, daughter of Pittheus, the king of Troezen. On a visit to

Troezen, Aegeus slept with Aethra, and she became pregnant, later giving birth to Theseus. Another story, however, emerged about Theseus's conception. According to this story, as Aethra was walking near the sea, the god Poseidon came out of the sea and had sex with her. Later, on the same night, she made her way to the bed of Aegeus. Was Theseus's father Aegeus or Poseidon? Given Theseus's later deeds, it seems that much of his power was derived from a divine parent, as was the case, for instance, with Herakles (Hercules) of the twelve labors; Perseus, the beheader of Medusa; and Achilles, the great warrior of Homer's *Iliad*, each of whom had a divine parent. In any case, Aegeus longed for a son to succeed him as king of Athens, and when he left to return home after his night with Aethra, he buried his favorite sandals and his sword under a rock and commanded Pittheus to instruct the son born to Aethra that when he became a man he should dig up the sandals and sword and travel to Athens, where Aegeus would recognize him because of the sandals and the sword.

Theseus as a young man does just that. On his way to Athens in search of his father, he establishes his hero credentials further by defeating monsters, outlaws, and other embodiments of evil threatening the people. These adventures or "labors" mirror those of the famous hero Herakles (Hercules), who much later will play a significant role in Theseus's life.

Arriving in Athens, Theseus's meeting with Aegeus is first prevented by the king's wife, the witch Medea, who had helped another hero, Jason, obtain the Golden Fleece and then was betrayed by him. Medea attempts to poison Theseus but is prevented from doing so when Aegeus recognizes the sword he had buried in Troezen and celebrates the young Theseus as his son and heir.

After this, Theseus has many heroic adventures, the most famous of which is his killing of the half human, half bull—Minotaur—in Crete. Because of a military defeat, Athens had made a treaty with Crete that involved Athenian youths being sent at regular intervals to Crete, where they would be eaten by the Minotaur in its labyrinth. With the help of Ariadne, a daughter of the Cretan king, Minos, Theseus, who has volunteered to be one of the youths so as to save his fellow Athenians, manages to kill the Minotaur and release the hostages.

In another adventure, Theseus descends to the underworld with a friend with the goal of releasing Persephone, the daughter of the earth goddess Demeter. Persephone had been abducted by and forced to marry the underworld god, Hades. The mission fails, however, and Theseus is trapped in the underworld until Herakles arrives on a mission of his own and releases him.

There are many more stories of the life of Theseus, not all successes. By mistake he even kills his own son, and in the end, he is exiled from Athens and thrown to his death from a cliff. Like many Greek heroes, Theseus is finally a "tragic hero," one of many such heroes who are protagonists, for instance, in the great tragic plays of Athens written by Aeschylus, Sophocles, and Euripides. In these plays, tragic heroes such as Agamemnon, Oedipus, and Theseus reflect the human fact that however noble and admirable one's deeds might be, they exist in the context of inevitable flaws and limitations (ultimately death) that separate humans from the gods.

Greece: Antigone

Most Greek heroes are male, reflecting an adamantly patriarchal culture. An exception is Antigone, the protagonist of the Sophocles play of that name. Like her father, Oedipus, she is a tragic hero, trapped in a dilemma that pitches morality against political reality. Antigone reflects the reality of "no way out," a familiar human dilemma.

Antigone's conception is not miraculous, but it is highly unusual, and it foreshadows a tragic fate. She is one of four children born to Oedipus and his mother-wife, Jocasta. Just as Antigone does not choose her situation, Oedipus had not realized until too late that the woman he had married was his mother. In the Greek view, it is the gods who control such events, using humans—even heroic ones—as pawns in a universal chess game.

Antigone's role in the game is complex. Her two brothers, Polynices and Eteocles, fought against each other for the throne of Thebes, their father's kingdom. The brothers managed to kill each other in the process, leading to the installation of their uncle, Creon, as king. Creon makes a political decision favoring Eteocles and decrees that he should be accorded normal religious burial rites while Poylnices should be refused the same rites. Antigone, who, as a loyal daughter, had accompanied her disgraced father, Oedipus, in his final years of wandering in blindness, defies the king by symbolically "burying" her brother by casting dirt on his rotting body. Her sister Ismene refuses to participate in Antigone's defiant act. She represents a more cautious and law-abiding, decidedly nonheroic, aspect of human nature. Caught in her law breaking, Antigone is brought before the king for judgment. Creon has made his pronouncement favoring one brother over the other for political reasons, to achieve order in his kingdom. Antigone has chosen to defy him on religious, moral, and family loyalty grounds. From Creon's point of view, he has no alternative but to condemn Antigone to death. Antigone has no choice but to bury her brother and accept death. Both protagonist and antagonist are wrong; both are right from their points of view. Antigone is placed in a walled-up place where she commits suicide. Creon is punished for his role in Antigone's tragedy when his son, who loves Antigone, joins her in her prison and ends his own life. As a hero, Antigone represents the flaw of pride (*hubris*) common to many heroes— perhaps all tragic heroes—but she also represents the aspect of human nature that places higher values before ordinary ones.

Celtic (Ireland): Cuchulainn

Like Theseus and many other mythic heroes, the Irish hero Cuchulainn is closely associated with his homeland and its history. His story is told in many legendary sources, especially in the prose epic the *Tain Bo Cuailnge* (The cattle raid of Cooley). Cuchulainn is one of the most complete of archetypal heroes. His conception is miraculous, one parent is a god, he proves himself as a child, performing amazing feats, his life is a quest marked by his prowess in many battles, and he even descends to and returns from the underworld.

There are many versions of Cuchulainn's conception. They all say his mother was Dechtire, the sister of King Conchobar of Ulster, and his father was the sun god Lugh, one of the Tuatha De Danann. In one story Dechtire is impregnated by Lugh when he takes the form of a fly and drops into a mug from which she drinks. When a boy is born to her, she names him Sentata. From a young age Sentata accomplishes great feats. As a seven-year-old he fights off an attack on King Conchobar's court. At the age of twelve he kills the great hound of Culann the smith and replaces the dog as Culann's protector, now taking the name Cuchulainn, meaning "Culann's hound."

Cuchulainn falls in love with the beautiful Emer and undergoes difficult trials to win her hand, including descending to and returning from the underworld. Cuchulainn's life is not without tragedy. Like the Greek hero Theseus, he kills his own son, albeit without realizing who he is. And he develops a rivalry with the powerful goddess Morrigan, whose advances he refuses scornfully, much as Gilgamesh, in the Babylonian version of his saga, spurns the great goddess Ishtar (formerly Inanna). The struggle with Morrigan will result in his death.

A central event in Cuchulainn's life is the great war of the *Tain* epic. In this war against the forces of Queen Medh (Maeve) of Connacht he reveals himself in all his demigod's power. Like Achilles in Homer's *Iliad* or the *berserkers* in Norse mythology, he becomes a superhuman beast in his battle fury. In one great battle he was said to have killed so many enemies that their bodies formed a wall around his army's camp.

But Cuchulainn, however heroic, is, like all heroes, human. One day he encounters an old woman washing his blood-stained armor in a stream. The old woman is, in fact, Morrigan, the armor is his, and the scene is an omen. With Morrigan's help, the young kings of Munster and Leinster, whose fathers had fallen victim to the hero's war fury, cornered Cuchulainn near a place known as the Pillar of Stone. Mortally wounded there, Cuchulainn ties himself to the pillar—some say with his own entrails—so that he can die on his feet. When a crow—actually Morrigan—lands on his shoulder, his enemies know the great Cuchulainn is finally dead.

Europe: King Arthur

Arthur Pendragon, or King Arthur, is believed by some to have been a Celtic (Briton) warrior who fought the Saxons in the fifth century CE. There are many other theories as well, but the historicity of King Arthur and his Round Table of questing knights is now largely dismissed. In fact, the King Arthur we know is the quasi-religious, sometimes mystical British hero of a complex mythology created by several authors, beginning with the Welsh monk Nennius, who in his 796 CE *Historia Brittonum* identifies Arthur as a Celtic war leader who fought the Saxons. It was the twelfth-century clergyman-historian Geoffrey of Monmouth, however, who, in his *Historia regnum Britanniae* (*History of the Kings of Britain*), began developing the myth of Arthur in earnest. Additions were contributed by the twelfth-century French Provencal poets Chretien de Troyes and Robert de Boron, and by the German poets Wolfram von Eschenback and Gottfried von Strassburg somewhat later. Elements were also added in the early thirteenth century by the Welsh writer Walter Map and, still later, in the fifteenth century, by Sir Thomas Mallory in his ever-popular English prose work (with a French title), *Le Morte d'Arthur*.

It is from these works combined that the archetypal hero emerges. Arthur's conception, if not miraculous, is at least magical. When

Uther (Uther Pendragon) was king of Britain, he fell in love with the beautiful Igraine, wife of the aging duke of Cornwall, one of the king's allies in the war against the invading Saxons. Uther was unable to conceal his ardent affection for Igraine. Displeased, the duke took his wife away to his impregnable castle in Tintagel. Desperate, Uther asked the master magician Merlin for help. Merlin used his powers to turn Uther into an exact copy of the duke, making it possible for him not only to enter the castle at Tintagel, but also to make Igraine believe he was her husband. On the night of Uther's arrival at Tintagel and Igraine's bed, Arthur was conceived. On the same night the duke of Cornwall was killed in battle.

Merlin predicted that one day Arthur would be a great king, and it was said that at his birth elves gave the baby special gifts of intelligence and power. In this way the future king's attachment to the supernatural or divine world was confirmed. Uther married Igraine and gave their child to a loyal knight, Sir Ector, to be raised. After Uther died, the kingdom seemed about to fall apart, so Merlin used more magic. He had the archbishop of Canterbury call together the nobles of the kingdom to decide on the succession to the throne. When the knights were assembled, a mysterious stone appeared, in it an embedded sword. Words written on the stone announced that whoever could pull the sword from the rock would be the rightful king. At Christmas and New Year various knights tried and failed to remove the sword. Then young Arthur arrived with Sir Ector and Sir Ector's son, Sir Kay, for whom Arthur acted as a squire-companion. When Sir Kay asked Arthur to return to their home to get his sword, Arthur noted that there was one in the stone, and he easily removed it and gave it to his foster brother. Sir Kay, now possessing the sword, demanded that he be named king. But Sir Ector insisted that to prove his worth, Sir Kay replace the sword in the stone and then remove it. Kay failed to remove the sword. Once again, Arthur removed it easily and was named king.

Later King Arthur established his Round Table of Knights—
Percival, Gawain, and others—heroes in their own right, who
undertook heroic quests, especially the quest for the Holy Grail,
the cup used by Jesus at the Last Supper, the Passover meal he
presided over the night before his death, and that a follower of
Jesus had brought to Britain.

According to some, it was Sir Galahad, a son of Sir Lancelot, who
succeeded in finding the Grail, although Sir Percival and Sir
Gawain at least saw it. After the Grail was found, the Round Table
broke up and a final battle ensued. In that battle many of the
knights were killed. As for Arthur himself, it was said by some that
he was killed by his son or nephew, Mordred, whose mother was
Arthur's half sister, the sorceress Morgan le Fay. But, in keeping
with the archetypal hero myth, Merlin claimed that Arthur was, in
fact, alive, that he had been taken to the mysterious island of
Avalon, and that, as the "once and future king," he would return
one day.

King Arthur remains a symbol of sacred sovereignty and of better
days to come.

Mesoamerica (Toltec/Aztec): Quetzalcoatl

Quetzalcoatl (Kukulkán to the Maya), the Feathered Serpent, was
a god of importance to all the pre-Columbian cultures of
Mesoamerica—particularly to the Toltec and Aztec peoples, in
whose mythologies he takes on characteristics of the archetypal
hero as well as that of a creator god. In the former context, his life
begins with a miraculous conception involving the virgin
Chimalman. There are many versions of the conception story.
In one, a god who takes the form of the Morning (Citlallatonac)
breathed on the virgin, and she conceived Quetzalcoatl, who at
birth was endowed with adult qualities of knowledge and wisdom.
As soon as she had performed her role as Quetzalcoatl's mother,
Chimalman died and went to heaven. In this she resembles the

Buddha's mother, Maha Maya, who died after serving as the vehicle for her son's arrival in the world.

Quetzalcoatl's later life is also reported in many versions, but all agree that he was sent by the gods to act as a culture hero, teaching the people such things as the arts and the calendar and giving them maize. Quetzalcoatl lived in a beautiful shining silver palace, and the people were happy until Quetzalcoatl's old enemy, Tezcatlipoca, the bearer of strife and pain, arrived. He challenged the hero to a game of ball, which all the people watched. During the game, Tezcatlipoca turned into a jaguar and attacked Quetzalcoatl, chasing him away from his home.

When Quetzalcoatl, now an old man, came to the sea, he sailed away on a raft of snakes. Some say he, like King Arthur, will return one day. Others say he ascended to heaven and became a star. Still others say that when the Spanish arrived in Mexico, the people mistook the conquistador Cortez as Quetzalcoatl, since the great hero was said to have been light skinned. The Aztecs paid dearly for their mistake.

Indonesia (Ceram): Hainuwele

Another sacrificial hero tale is that of the Ceramese maiden Hainuwele, whose life is marked by several characteristics of the archetypal hero, including the miraculous conception, the descent to death, and the resurrection and return with a great boon for the people. According to the story, there was a man named Ameta, who took his dog hunting one day. When the dog picked up the scent of a wild pig, Ameta followed him to a pond into which the pig fled and where it eventually drowned. When Ameta fished the dead pig out of the water it had a coconut caught on its snout. This was the first coconut on the earth.

So Ameta took the pig and the coconut home. There he wrapped the coconut in a cloth as if it were a baby, and he planted it. Three weeks later there was a coconut palm plant there, and soon it grew into a full palm tree. One day Ameta cut himself by mistake, and some of his blood fell on a palm leaf. In a few days a baby girl emerged from the blood, and in a few more days she had become the beautiful Hainuwele, who gave many good things to her people, acting as a culture hero.

Then came the day of the Maro Dance in which all nine families of the people participated. Tied together by a rope, the men and women encircled the generous Hainuwele and danced closer and closer to her until finally they pushed her into the pit at the center of the circle. The dancers drowned out the girl's cries, and they packed the earth over her.

After killing and planting Hainuwele, the people experienced death. After being killed, Hainuwele built a huge gate at one of the dancing places, and from that time on, the people had to die and pass through that gate to go to the underworld to see Hainuwele. Meanwhile, from the place where she was buried, the tubers emerged that are the peoples' staple diet. Hainuwele has mythical relatives in other heroes such as Corn Mother and Jesus, who are miraculously conceived, suffer ritual sacrifices, and arise as sustenance for their people.

The hero and us

What stands out in the hero's life is that it is, finally, a human life. Heroes often have a divine parent, but they nearly always have a human one as well. Heroes have extraordinary, often supernatural, powers and support, but they wear the human clothes of flesh and blood. Their extraordinary acts are metaphors for our condition. They struggle against the very concept of death, they search for their identity, they struggle against their monsters. Whether culture heroes like Hainuwele or Corn Mother, questing heroes like King Arthur and his knights or Gilgamesh, tragic heroes like

Antigone and Oedipus, monster slayers like Theseus and Herakles or St. George, or religious culture heroes, like the Buddha, Zoroaster, Moses, and Jesus, heroes exist to explore the extremes of human possibility. They overcome the limitations of their cultures and break new ground for the life experience.

World mythology and cultural myths

The defining characteristic of human beings may well be our ability to conceive of plot (what Aristotle called *mythos*)—that is, of narratives with beginnings, middles, and ends. By extension, humans, unlike other animal species, think and act in relation to the past, the present, and the future. Another way of putting this is to suggest that a primary, if not *the* primary, role of humans on earth is to make creation conscious of itself. Paleolithic cave paintings in places like Lascaux in France and myths told orally in all parts of the world and later written down reveal a human need to describe and explain the world in narratives. Behind these narratives are several universal human questions. Where did we come from? Did someone create us? Are we sometimes punished by that being? Why is there evil in the world? Do we have a way of breaking out of the limitations on our lives?

How these questions are answered depends on the cultures that answer them. World mythology is a collection of cultural mythologies, each as different from each other as their parent cultures are different. Cultural identification is related to such matters as physical environment, religion, living arrangements, and traditions. To come to life, myths require cultural details. Greek mythology is what it is because of Greek culture. Sumerian mythology clearly reflects the details of Sumerian culture. That said, there are certain elements or motifs that exist in nearly all cultural mythologies and that can be said to transcend cultures. These include the five myth concepts discussed in this book. The concepts of deity, creation, and the hero are universal. Those of the flood and the trickster are so common as to be almost so. It is also fair to say that within the cultural expressions of these concepts are motifs or narrative structures that cross many cultural barriers. The hero's quest is an example, as are the cosmic egg in creation and the presence of a creator deity. To discuss these universal concepts and common motifs is to discuss world mythology in a sense that is somewhat different from the sense of world mythology as simply a collection of cultural mythologies. The myths collected in this book represent both senses of world mythology.

The first deities of which we have written records are those of Sumer and Egypt. Archeological evidence suggests that deities were worshipped long before the invention of writing. Sites such as Çatal Hüyük and Hacilar in Anatolia contain sculptural evidence of deities, including shrines with apparent goddess and animal god figures, dating to about 7000 BCE, and several famous figurines such as the tiny Venus of Willendorf suggest the belief in a fertility goddess much earlier than that.

The belief in deities remains strong despite an absence of clear signals from them. Although there are many myths of gods speaking directly with people, these are stories of events that took place long ago, events that people rarely expect to happen again soon. In short, if deities exist, they resist open and transparent communication with humans. Nevertheless, humans continue, through elaborate structures, complex rituals, and various types of prayer, to attempt to maintain contact with them.

Humans do not like to be isolated, either physically or psychologically. To exist as a child without a family, without a father and a mother, is to be left in a random state in a threatening place. The same is true of cultures. For a given culture to survive as a culture requires a sense of security that comes from being created, watched over, and recognized by a reality outside of and more powerful than itself. Naturally enough, cultures always imagine this reality in human terms—as fathers, mothers, and families—gods, goddesses, and pantheons. These deities and their families can be benevolent like the Navajo Yeii, distant and aloof like the Egyptian gods, strict and rule demanding like the Hebrew Yahweh, intimate like the Sumerian Inanna, intellectual and hard to understand like the Indian gods, or even arbitrary, selfish, and fickle, like the Greek Olympians. To a great extent, the perceived nature of the deities in question depends on the nature and conditions of the worlds in which they have brought up their "children." This is where creation myths become important.

We are all curious about the sources of our individual existence—our parents, our older ancestors—and the circumstances of our births. This information can affect our lives in terms of such elements as class, ethnicity, and relationship to place. Our personal origin stories establish our life credentials. The same is true of cultures. In its creation myth a culture establishes its sacred lineage, its unique relation to deities, its place in existence, and, by extension, its sense of itself in terms of status and purpose.

While the establishment of sacred history through creation myths is common to all cultures, the details of the histories vary radically according to environment and life conditions. The ancient Egyptians, for instance, were a proud culture dominated by the great pharaohs—the builders of pyramids and sphynxes—and by the fertility provided by the Nile to an otherwise barren and sun-baked desert. The Egyptian creation myths establish close—even intimate—connections between Egypt, fertility, and the Creator. According to the priests of Heliopolis, the creation of their world was initiated ex nihilo by the flowing of bodily fluids—semen, sweat, saliva, or tears—from the great god Atum himself. Other cultures have other stories celebrating their sacred origins. The Dogon people trace their cultural significance and the sacredness of their individual bodies to a cosmic egg sent by the Creator. Native Americans tend to have creation myths that stress their creation from Mother Earth rather than from heavenly deities.

Naturally enough, many cultures envision creation in the terms of human reproduction. In these myths, world parents—generally representing earth and sky—constantly pressed together, must be separated by their children to allow space for life between them for further creation. Rangi and Papa in Polynesia, An and Ki in Sumer, and Gaia and Ouranos and Kronos and Rhea in Greece are examples. The separation of the world parents might well reflect the negative reactions of many children to the sexual relations of their parents—a parental union that excludes them. But it also establishes cultures in which old gods and "primitive" forces of nature were overpowered by new gods and their dynasties, reflecting the rise of more centralized cultures that replaced older ones, as in the cases of Sumer and Greece. A more violent form of the separation myth involves the sacrifice of a primitive being who becomes the building material of a new world. Thus, Marduk defeats the ancient world parent Tiamat and uses her body parts to build the new Babylonian world of which he is the national god. And Aesir gods use the body of the ancient monster Ymir as the building materials of their new world. The Aztecs have a similar creation myth. Whatever the nature of a given culture's creation myth, the myth establishes a sacred reason for the culture's existence.

But what if a culture betrays the sacred lineage celebrated in its creation myth? Since the history of the world is a history of such betrayals, it is not surprising that we have myths in which the creator deity addresses the problem. The solution is to destroy the world and then give it a second chance. The most common instrument for world destruction is a flood. As a nearly universal archetype in many iterations, the flood myth in one sense can be seen as a projection of human guilt over our corruption and

111

betrayal of creation. In this sense, flood myths function essentially as stories of productive sacrifice. The world as we know it must be sacrificed to make a new world possible. The deluge cleans even as it kills. As in many creation myths, the world emerges from primordial maternal waters; in the flood we experience a second birth. The humans spared in the flood myth—Noah, Manu, Utnapishtim, Deucalion and Pyrrah, and others—are projections of the possibility of a new world.

As flood myths respond to the human betrayal of creation, however, they say little about the reasons for that betrayal and the perseverance of human corruption in the post-flood age. What was it in a presumably perfect creation that caused the betrayal? For most of us, the answer lies in human nature itself—human selfishness, human greed, human appetites, perceived human needs. A mythic projection of these characteristics within human nature is the trickster.

In many cultural iterations, the trickster (almost always he rather than she) commits outrageous, antisocial deeds. The Native Americans Coyote and Iktome are ruthless in their predatorial treatment of women and their willingness to cheat and steal to satisfy their appetites. They express the animal rather than the spiritual aspects of human nature. Other tricksters, such as the Egyptian Set and the Norse Loki, are more overtly evil. Set works against Isis and the young Horus, Loki contributes to the destruction of the Aesir, and the biblical serpent corrupts Adam and Eve and their Garden of Eden. The central Asian tricksters and sometimes the Native American ones try to undermine the Creator's fashioning of human beings with bogus creations of their own that represent an inherently corrupted humanity.

But the trickster, like human nature, is ambiguous. Sometimes his deeds are committed in the interest of humanity, for whom he even acts as a culture hero. As he represents negative aspects of human nature, he is also nearly always an embodiment of the aspect of that nature that works to break through the barriers of conventionality and the dominance of arbitrary authority. The Sumerian Enki, for all his incestuous and uncontrolled sexuality, is a source of his world's fertility. The African tricksters Legba and Ananse trick their creators to gain necessary boons for their people. Even the biblical serpent can be seen as a hero of sorts, as he leads the otherwise unthinking first couple to the Tree of Knowledge of Good and Evil, freeing them from the bounds of ignorance.

If, as some scholars have suggested, the trickster stands for our preconscious, amoral, but creative animal state, the hero represents the drive within us that struggles against the forces resistant to spiritual and humanistic advancement. Whatever the parentage or extraordinary powers of the hero, he or she is the element of mythology that most closely represents our adherence to the concept of life as a meaningful plot with a beginning, middle, and end. The hero is our persona in world mythology, the symbol of whatever it is we strive for in life.

More than the deity, creation, flood, and trickster myths, hero myths lend themselves to a comparative approach. Even for those dismissive of that approach, it is difficult to deny the presence of certain archetypal patterns in the hero myths. The pattern begins with a conception and/or birth that clearly marks the individual in question as a special person. Quetzalcoatl and Jesus are born of virgins, the Navajo twin heroes are conceived when the sun lingers briefly on the body of Changing Woman, Abraham's son Isaac is born of an ancient and presumably barren woman, the Virgin Mary is herself immaculately conceived, Hainuwele and Cuchulainn are conceived miraculously, the Buddha and Guanyin are conceived in dreams, Draupadi is born of fire, and Gilgamesh, Theseus, Cuchulainn, Quetzalcoatl, and Jesus all have at least one divine parent.

Birth, by definition, expresses the hope for a new beginning. Born of maternal waters, the hero mirrors the emergence from the

113

primordial waters in so many creation myths. The fact that heroes are born outside the "normal" process suggests that they belong not to any one family but to a whole culture. The hero's role in life will be to reach beyond normality to achieve something that reflects a culture's longing for a higher goal. Through the unusual conception and birth, the hero carries the divine essence through a mother's doorway into the human world.

The hero is almost always threatened—usually from an early age—by forces that see the heroic presence as a threat to its existence. Moses is threatened by Pharaoh, Jesus by Herod, Zoroaster by King Duransarun, the Buddha by Mara the Fiend, Quetzalcoatl by Tezcatlipoca, Antigone by Creon, Guanyin by her father, the king. With some divine help, the hero overcomes what is essentially conventional, if evil, obstructionism. The hero's call to adventure—the quest—is stronger than any mere king. This is not to say that the hero's quest is always successful. Gilgamesh seeks eternal life and fails; Antigone, like many tragic heroes, seeks religious justice and dies; Quetzalcoatl loses in his quest for order and prosperity for his people; Draupadi suffers in her superhuman acts of fidelity; Theseus kills the Minotaur but never finds peace in his life; Jesus dies on the cross; Moses never gets to the Promised Land.

The hero quest tells us that it is the quest itself, not its success, that is significant. Like the hero, we cannot achieve eternal life or any kind of perfection, but it is the attempt to get there that is heroic and that connects the hero to us and our lives, both our external and internal lives. It is the Buddha's search for enlightenment rather than his realization of it that make him heroic. It is the trials of King Arthur and his knights rather than the finding of the Holy Grail that make the king and his knights heroic symbols of the possibilities of human achievement. The hero's quest, with its descent to the underworld, its monster slaying, its search for the likes of the Holy Grail or Golden Fleece, is a metaphor for our own ideals and aspirations, our own dealings with death, with arbitrary barriers to our wholeness, and our own psychological monsters.

World mythology, then, is a collection of the many ways in which humans have projected the journey of life. Our deities reflect the hope that we are not alone, that there is a reason for our existence. Creation myths give significance to our world and our lives in it. Flood and trickster myths express our failures and reasons for them. Hero myths are expressions of human hope and human pride and determination.

Further reading

Andersen, Johannes C. *Myths and Legends of the Polynesians.*
New York: Dover, 2011.

Aston, W. G., trans. *Nihongi: Chronicles of Japan from the Earliest of Times to A.D. 697.* North Clarendon, VT: Tuttle, 2011.

Bierhorst, John. *The Mythology of South America.* New York: William Morrow, 1985.

Campbell, Joseph. *The Hero with a Thousand Faces.* Princeton, NJ: Princeton University Press, 1968.

Dundes, Alan, ed. *The Flood Myth.* Berkeley: University of California Press, 1988.

Eliade, Mircea, ed. *The Encyclopedia of Religion.* New York: Macmillan, 1986.

Euripides. *The Bacchae and Other Plays.* Translated by James Morwood. Oxford: Oxford University Press, 2000.

Fee, Christopher. *Arthur: God and Hero in Avalon.* London: Reaktion, 2019.

Fee, Christopher, and David A. Leeming. *The Goddess: Myths of the Great Mother.* London: Reaktion, 2016.

Fee, Christopher, with David A. Leeming. *Gods, Heroes, and Kings: The Battle for Mythic Britain.* New York: Oxford University Press, 2001.

Freeman, Philip. *Celtic Mythology: Tales of Gods, Goddesses, and Heroes.* New York: Oxford University Press, 2017.

George, Andrew, trans. *The Epic of Gilgamesh.* London: Penguin, 2003.

Goetz, Della, Sylvanus G. Morley, and Adrian Recion, trans. *Popol Vuh: The Sacred Book of the Ancient Quiche Maya.* Norman: University of Oklahoma Press, 1991.

Hansen, William. *Classical Mythology: A Guide to the Mythical World of the Greeks and Romans.* 2nd ed. New York: Oxford University Press, 2020.

Heldt, Gustav, trans. *The Kojiki: An Account of Ancient Matters.* New York: Columbia University Press, 2014.

Hyde, Lewis. *Trickster Makes the World: Mischief, Myth, and Art.* New York: Farrar, Straus and Giroux, 2010.

Jung, C. G., and C. Kerenyi. *Essays on a Science of Mythology: The Myth of the Divine Child and the Mysteries of Eleusis.* Princeton, NJ: Princeton University Press (Bollingen), 1963.

Kinsella, Thomas, trans. *The Tain.* Oxford: Oxford University Press, 1970.

Kramer, Samuel Noah. *Sumerian Mythology.* Rev. ed. Philadelphia: University of Pennsylvania Press, 1998.

Leeming, David A. *Creation Myths of the World: An Encyclopedia.* 2 vols. Santa Barbara, CA: ABC-CLIO, 2010.

Leeming, David A. *A Dictionary of Asian Mythology.* New York: Oxford University Press, 2001.

Leeming, David A. *From Olympus to Camelot: The World of European Mythology.* New York: Oxford University Press, 2003.

Leeming, David A. *Jealous Gods and Chosen People: The Mythology of the Middle East.* New York: Oxford University Press, 2004.

Leeming, David A. *Mythology: The Voyage of the Hero.* 3rd ed. New York: Oxford University Press, 1998.

Leeming, David A. *The Oxford Companion to World Mythology.* New York: Oxford University Press, 2005.

Leeming, David A. *Sex in the World of Myth.* London: Reaktion, 2018.

Leeming, David A. *Tales of the Earth: Native North American Creation Mythology.* London: Reaktion, 2021.

Leeming, David A. *The World of Myth.* Rev. ed. New York: Oxford University Press, 2013.

Leeming, David A., and Jake Page. *God: Myths of the Male Divine.* New York: Oxford University Press, 1996.

Leeming, David A., and Jake Page. *Goddess: Myths of the Female Divine.* New York: Oxford University Press, 1994.

Leeming, David A., and Jake Page. *The Mythology of Native North America.* Norman: University of Oklahoma Press, 1998.

Lindow, John. *Norse Mythology: A Guide to the Gods, Heroes, Rituals, and Beliefs.* New York: Oxford University Press, 2001.

Lynch, Patricia Ann. *African Mythology A to Z.* New York: Facts on File, 2004.

Narayan, R. K., trans. *The Mahabharata: A Shortened Prose Version*. Chicago: University of Chicago Press, 2016.

Pinch, Geraldine. *Egyptian Mythology: A Guide to the Gods, Goddesses, and Traditions of Ancient Egypt*. New York: Oxford University Press, 2002.

Radin, Paul. *The Trickster: A Study in Native American Mythology*. New York: Schocken, 1956.

Raglan, Lord Fitzroy. *The Hero: A Study in Tradition, Myth, and Drama*. 1856. Drama. [1956] Mineola, NY: Dover 2011.

Rank, Otto. *The Myth of the Birth of the Hero and Other Writings*. Edited by Philip Freund. New York: Random House, 1956.

Read, Kay Almere, and Jason J. Gonzalez. *Mesoamerican Mythology: A Guide to the Gods, Heroes, Rituals, and Beliefs of Mexico and Central America*. New York: Oxford University Press, 2000.

Segal, Robert. *Myth: A Very Short Introduction*. Oxford: Oxford University Press, 2004.

Smith, W. Ramsay. *Myths and Legends of the Australian Aborigines*. New York: Dover, 2003.

Sturluson, Snorri. *The Prose Edda: Norse Mythology*. Translated by Jesse L. Byock. London: Penguin Classics, 2006.

Williams, George M. *Handbook of Hindu Mythology*. New York: Oxford University Press, 2003.

Wolkstein, Diane, and Samuel Noah Kramer. *Inanna: Queen of Heaven and Earth*. New York: Harper & Row, 1983.

Yang, Lihui, Deming An, and Jessica Anderson Turner. *Handbook of Chinese Mythology*. New York: Oxford University Press. 2008.

Index

Index

World Mythology

H

CLASSICAL MYTHOLOGY
A Very Short Introduction
Helen Morales

From Zeus and Europa, to Diana, Pan, and Prometheus, the myths of ancient Greece and Rome seem to exert a timeless power over us. But what do those myths represent, and why are they so enduringly fascinating? This imaginative and stimulating *Very Short Introduction* is a wide-ranging account, examining how classical myths are used and understood in both high art and popular culture, taking the reader from the temples of Crete to skyscrapers in New York, and finding classical myths in a variety of unexpected places: from Arabic poetry and Hollywood films, to psychoanalysis, the bible, and New Age spiritualism.

WITCHCRAFT
A Very Short Introduction
Malcolm Gaskill

Witchcraft is a subject that fascinates us all, and everyone knows
what a witch is - or do they? From childhood most of us develop a
sense of the mysterious, malign person, usually an old woman.
Historically, too, we recognize witch-hunting as a feature of pre-
modern societies. But why do witches still feature so heavily in our
cultures and consciousness? From Halloween to superstitions,
and literary references such as Faust and even Harry Potter,
witches still feature heavily in our society. In this Very Short
Introduction Malcolm Gaskill challenges all of this, and argues
that what we think we know is, in fact, wrong.

'Each chapter in this small but perfectly-formed book could be the
jumping-off point for a year's stimulating reading. Buy it now.'

Fortean Times